Aurignacian Clay Hearths from Klissoura Cave 1

An experimental approach

Małgorzata Kot

BAR International Series 2331

2012

Published in 2016 by
BAR Publishing, Oxford

BAR International Series 2331

Aurignacian Clay Hearths from Klissoura Cave 1

ISBN 978 1 4073 0914 9

BAR Publishing is the trading name of British Archaeological Reports (Oxford) Ltd.
British Archaeological Reports was first incorporated in 1974 to publish the BAR
Series, International and British. In 1992 Hadrian Books Ltd became part of the BAR
group. This volume was originally published by Archaeopress in conjunction with
British Archaeological Reports (Oxford) Ltd / Hadrian Books Ltd, the Series principal
publisher, in 2012. This present volume is published by BAR Publishing, 2016.

Printed in England

BAR
PUBLISHING

BAR titles are available from:

BAR Publishing
122 Banbury Rd, Oxford, OX2 7BP, UK
EMAIL   info@barpublishing.com
PHONE   +44 (0)1865 310431
FAX   +44 (0)1865 316916
www.barpublishing.com

TABLE OF CONTENTS

ACKNOWLEDGEMENTS 3

LIST OF FIGURES... 4

INTRODUCTION 5

CHAPTER 1 DESCRIPTION OF THE CLAY HEARTHS.. 6

CHAPTER 2 METHODOLOGY OF THE EXPERIMENTS.. 8

CHAPTER 3 FIRST SERIES OF EXPERIMENTS 11

CHAPTER 4 SECOND SERIES OF EXPERIMENTS 13

CHAPTER 5 THIRD SERIES OF EXPERIMENTS... 18

CHAPTER 6 FOURTH SERIES OF EXPERIMENTS.. 28

CHAPTER 7 RESULTS.. 53

CHAPTER 8 CONCLUSIONS: THE USES OF THE CLAY HEARTHS 57

BIBLIOGRAPHY.. 61

ACKNOWLEDGEMENTS

In the first place I would like to thank the Consultative Council on the University of Warsaw's Student Scientific Movement for granting my project. I am thankful to Academy Artes Liberales, which enabled me to take classes on the Jagiellonian University.

I would like to express my gratitude to Professor Janusz Kozłowski, Professor Bolesław Ginter and Associated Professor Krzysztof Sobczyk, from Jagiellonian University who inspired me to start the project and generously made available information additional to that originally contained in preliminary reports. I am very thankful for my supervisor Professor Karol Szymczak, PhD (Warsaw University) for the encouragement he gave me to keep the project going. I thank Margarita Koumouzelis (Ephoreia of Palaeoanthropology-Speleology in Athens) who helped me with conducting experiments in Greece. I particularly benefited from many discussions with Panagiotis Karkanas (Ephoreia of Palaeoanthropology-Speleology in Athens) who gave me invaluable assistance and advice on all geological and petrographical matters. I am particularly grateful to Professor Dragos Gheorghiu (National University of Arts in Bucharest) who enables me to conduct a series of experiments in Centre of Experimental Archaeology in Vadastra providing me with termocouples which changed the entire project. I am very thankful for Maria Rosa Albert, PhD (University of Barcelona) for helpful remarks and a discussion.

I am grateful to Mrs. Anna Kinecka for a translation, to Jan Skupiński for the proofreading. I thank Maciej Biłas who helped me with redrafting the diagrams and graphs and invaluable assistance on editing the text. Finally, but by no means least I would like to thank my mother for the help, understanding, and support she constantly gave throughout this time.

3

LIST OF FIGURES

Fig. 2.1 Scheme of a distribution of the measuring points..9

Fig. 4.1 Scheme of the first cycle of experiments including p1KII, p2KII and p3KII....................13

Fig. 4.2 Scheme of the second cycle of experiments including p4KII, p5KII and p6KII.................13

Fig. 5.1 Scheme of the first cycle of experiments including p1RIII, p3RIII and p4RIII.................18

Fig. 5.2 Schemes of (a) the second cycle of experiments including p5RIII and p6RIII; (b) the third cycle of experiments including j1RIII and p7RIII. 19

Fig. 5.3 Temperature distribution in form p1RIII during a) the first firing episode; b) the second firing episode; c) the third firing episode including temperature distribution in forms p4RIII. 20

Fig. 5.4 Temperature distribution in form p3RIII during a) the first firing episode; b) second firing episode; c) third firing episode. 21

Fig. 5.5 Temperature distribution in form p5RIII during the first firing episode. 22

Fig. 5.6 Temperature distribution in form p6RIII during the first firing episode 23

Fig. 5.7 Temperature distribution in form p7RIII during a) the first firing episode; b) the second firing episode. 24

Fig. 5.8 A combined diagram of temperature distribution of forms p1RIII, p3RIII, p5RIII and p7RIII during a) the first firing episode; b) the second firing episode. 25

Fig. 5.9 A combined diagram of temperature distribution in T2 point of p3RIII during the first, the second and the third firing episode. 26

Fig. 6.1 Scheme of the first cycle of experiments including p1KIV, p2IV, p4KIV, p5KIV, p6KIV and p7KIV.............28

Fig. 6.2 Scheme of the second cycle of experiments including p3KIV and p10KIV. 28

Fig. 6.3 Scheme of the fourth cycle of experiments including P8KIV and p9KIV. 29

Fig. 6.4 Temperature distribution in form p1KIV during the first firing episode. 29

Fig. 6.5 Temperature distribution in form p2KIV during a) the first firing episode, b) the second firing episode, c) the third firing episode d) the fourth firing episode......................................31

Fig. 6.6 A combined diagram of temperature distribution in form p2KIV during all the firing episodes. 32

Fig. 6.7 Temperature distribution in form p5KIV during a) the first firing episode, b) the second firing episode, c) the third firing episode. 34

Fig. 6.8 A combined diagram of temperature distribution in form p5KIV during all the firing episodes. 36

Fig. 6.9 Temperature distribution in form p6KIV during a) the first firing episode, b) the second firing episode, c) the third firing episode d) the fourth firing episode 37

Fig. 6.10 A combined diagrams of temperature distribution in form p6KIV during all the firing episodes.....................39

Fig. 6.11 A combined diagram of the rate of temperature increase in form p6KIV during all firing episodes. 40

Fig. 6.12 Temperature distribution in form p10KIV during a) the first firing episode, b) the second firing episode, c) the third firing episode 43

Fig. 6.13 A combined diagram of the rate of temperature increase in form p10KIV during all firing episodes. 44

Fig. 6.14 A combined diagram of temperature distribution in form p10KIV during all the firing episodes 44

Fig. 6.15 A combined diagram of temperature distribution of forms p1KIV, p2KIV, p5KIV and p6KIV during a) the first firing; b) the second firing...47

Fig. 6.16 A combined diagram of temperature distribution of forms fired by embers and fire. 48

Fig. 6.17 A comparison of the average temperature during four firing episodes..49

Fig. 7.1 A combined diagram of temperature distribution of forms fired by embers and fire. 54

Fig. 8.1 General *chaîne opératoire* for the clay forms...58

Fig. 8.2 Schemes showing hypothetical ways of using clay structures. a) schemes without firing clay structures before using them, b) the schemes with firing the clay structure before using..59

INTRODUCTION

Clay was used on a wider scale starting from the Neolithic age. Evidences of its use during the Palaeolithic are rare. And thus, from the Older Stone Age we know of clay figurines of humans and animals (Vandiver, et al., 1989, Hachi, et al., 2002). Interesting phenomenons are also two hearths or stove–like features discovered at the site in Dolni Vestonice (Vandiver, et al., 1989). These features modelled from clay most probably represent the setting of hearths which were found within structures used as dwellings. So far from the period of the Palaeolithic only these two hearth features from the site Dolni Vestonice were known and considered together with animal figurines discovered in their vicinity as the oldest evidence on the use of fired clay by man. This situation was changed by research carried out at site Klissoura Cave 1 in the Peloponnese in Greece (Koumouzelis, et al., 2001a, 2001b). At site Klissoura 1, layers dated to the Upper Palaeolithic yielded a total of around 100 concave clay hearths. These forms were marked by having a circular outline and deep rust–red hue. Over most of these structures there was a layer of ashes. Analyses of clay samples show that the rust–hued structures are made of heated clay (Pawlikowski, et al., 2000, Karkanas, et al., 2004; Karkanas, 2010). Recurrence of this type of form over the small surface of the entire trench across the depth of in nearly two metres and quite regular shape suggest that they these features are man made.

Klissoura is a multi–layered site with layers dating back to the Middle Palaeolithic. In the Aurignacian layer were found concave clay forms which are estimated, by C14 dates, to be 35–37,5 calibrated kyrs BP (Kuhn, et al., 2010:39). The preliminary reports yielded a 114 whole or fragmented clay forms (Karkanas, et al., 2004:514–515), known as clay hearths. The most recent articles claim at least 80 clay hearths and multiple hearths with clay remains (Kaczanowska, Kozłowski and Sobczyk, 2010). They are frequently placed very close to one another or even one on top of the other. Above almost each of the clay hearths there is an ash layer which can be seen in the profile (Karkanas, 2010:25). Clay hearths are concave and round forms always found horizontally within the layer. It looks as if they were formed by filling a small hollow in the ground with a 2–6 centimetre layer of clay (Karkanas, et al. 2004:516). To form the clay hearths only clay with a natural admixture of quartz was used, with no additional admixture of sand, rubble, etc. These forms are typically 0.3–0.4 up to 0,7 metre in diameter (Karkanas, et al., 2004:515; Pawlikowski, et al., 2000:19; Kaczanowska, Kozłowski and Sobczyk, 2010) and light brown in cross–section. Petrographic analyses have shown that the clay hearths were exposed to high temperature, however, not exceeding 650°C (Pawlikowski, et al., 2000:23), although Karkanas established the temperature to be in the range of 400 to 600°C (2004:521; 2010:25).

Archaeologists still have not determined the purpose served by the clay hearths or how they were produced and burnt. It was suggested in one study that the remains of wild grass seeds identified in the ash layer above one of the clay hearths may be an evidence on the use of clay hearths for roasting wild grass seeds (Pawlikowski, et al., 2000:28; Karkanas, et al., 2004:522).

The subject matter of the project are clay hearths discovered at the Klissoura site. The book is a result of a 3–year project in experimental archaeology. The main issue of the project was the reconstruction of the whole process of making, firing and using Upper Palaeolithic clay hearths. The experiments were held in Centre of Experimental Archaeology in Biskupin (Poland), Centre of Experimental Archaeology, Museumsdorf Düppel (Germany), Centre of Experimental Archaeology in Vadastra (Romania) and nearby the Klissoura Cave 1 (Greece).

The author undertook to make an in–depth analysis of the clay hearths discovered at Klissoura to determine their purpose. This was done by developing a comprehensive catalogue of the clay hearth finds and subsequently by comparing the metric parameters of these structures in within individual archaeological levels. As a next step analysis was made of the spatial distribution of the clay hearths in the context of other archaeological features. The third stage involved the carrying out of archaeological experiments to determine the techniques of execution, possible firing and methods of using the clay hearths by Upper Palaeolithic people. Basing on research and results of analysis of animal and plant micro–and macro–remains the author developed few hypotheses on the possible uses of the concave clay hearths at site Klissoura.

CHAPTER 1

DESCRIPTION OF THE CLAY HEARTHS

Introduction

The concave layers of rust–hued clay discovered at site Klissoura Cave 1 are referred to in this paper interchangeably as 'clay forms', 'clay hearths' and 'clay structures'.

The clay hearths at the time of their discovery were in a state of nearly full disintegration. On most occasions the extent of the clay hearth was hard to detect and its surface could not be extracted. No traces of finger impressions or of working the clay into the concave shape could be seen on the surface of the clay. The clay forms, while being explored, were visible on the plan of the trench as circular rust–coloured discolourations which, as time passed, became reduced in their diameter and finally became solid circles. Only a very precise exploration made it possible to extract and lift a number of clay hearths entirely from the ground but after drying they disintegrated into many very small fragments (Karkanas, et al., 2004). The clay from the clay hearths, when wetted, formed a plastic mass and losing its original shape.
When discovered the forms survived only in their base section. Only a single clay hearth retained a fragment of its rim. This was the youngest of the features (Pawlikowski, et al., 2001). Most often the clay hearths survived in the form of flat rust–coloured lenses. Only in the case of the better preservation it was possible to distinguish their bottom from their sides and determine the how deep the form was.

Spatial Distribution

The clay hearths occurred in layers, which had a total thickness of over 1.8m. They6 were found in two sequences, of which sequence E represented the Lower Aurignacian level and sequence D represents the Middle Aurignacian, epi–Ulizzian and Backed Bladelet Industry levels (Kaczanowska, Kozłowski and Sobczyk, 2010). Looking in general at the number of forms within individual layers and sequences distinguished one notes that clay hearths concentrate mainly in the Lower Aurignacian layers (sequence E) (Kaczanowska, Kozłowski and Sobczyk, 2010: 198–199).

At the same time, analysis of spatial distribution of clay hearths within the trench shows a change of the location of the greatest concentration of these forms which is observed between clay hearths found within the Lower Aurignacian level (sequence E) and the uppermost levels (sequence D). While the first group was found near the walls of the cave, by the N profile of the trench, those discovered within the higher lying layers occurred by the S margin of the trench, and as such, farther away from the cave wall (Kaczanowska, Kozłowski and Sobczyk, 2010; Karkanas, 2010:30).

Two types of hearths were identified at the site. The first of these are hearths without traces of stone or clay structures as a rule with a substantial diameter. The other type are fires which had a clay hearth under a layer of ash. They tended to be smaller in diameter (25–40cm) (Kaczanowska, Kozłowski and Sobczyk, 2010). The occurrence of these two types of hearths suggests that each type served a different purpose. While the first group may be treated as all–purpose family hearths, around which the people would gather and prepare food, the smaller hearths probably had a different, quite specific purpose.

A spatial relationship between the family hearths and the hearths with a concave clay form was observed in three cases. The authors explained the described relationship by the necessity of moving the embers from the regular hearth into the clay hearth (Karkanas, et al., 2004; Karkanas, 2010:33). In the family hearth ashes and embers were produced and were later placed within the clay hearth. This type of relationship cannot be ruled out and is made all the more feasible by the spatial arrangement of the hearths.

On several occasions one clay hearth directly overlies another one of this kind (Karkanas, 2010: Fig.5,7,13; Kaczanowska, Kozłowski and Sobczyk, 2010: Fig.3). The occurrence of this type of structures indicates that the location where the clay hearth had been positioned was important and something not to be departed from. Perhaps the effect of superimposition of a clay hearth over the previous one enhanced its properties, for instance made the structure retain heat better. This practice suggests that the earlier clay hearth had deteriorated and ceased to serve its purpose. Consequently, the process must have been guided by some criteria of usefulness of this type of structure. Perhaps the cracked condition of a clay hearth was one such criterion. With regard to the occurrence of clay hearths established one over the other it is hard to say whether consequently the structures which occur next to each other are coterminous and were in parallel use or were set up in succession as the earlier forms were used up or became broken.

The existence of continuity of clay hearth locations, which is visible when we look at the frequency of occurrence of the clay hearths within individual grid squares and levels (Kaczanowska, Kozłowski and Sobczyk, 2010), suggests the existence of some notion of spatial organisation of such locations and that for some reason some places were considered as better for installing the clay hearth than others.

On the basis of the distribution of the fires and stones we may conclude that:

- The fires with clay hearths had a specific function (Meignen, et al. 2001) and were not household hearths positioned at the centre of the camping site.

They were mostly sited on the margin of the utility space under the cave walls.

- The location at a small distance from the cave walls may have been caused by the wish to shelter them from the wind and give them a roof as the cave walls in front of the cave form a sort of a awning which today reaches more or less to the middle of the trench (ca. 2 metres from the entrance to the cave) (Kaczanowska, Kozłowski and Sobczyk, 2010:143).
- It cannot be ruled out that the fires with clay hearths were always established next to a fire without a clay hearth, which e.g. was used for producing embers.

CHAPTER 2

METHODOLOGY OF THE EXPERIMENTS

Introduction

As it was stressed before the occurrence of two types of hearths at the site suggests that each type served a different purpose. While non–structure hearths may be treated as all–purpose family hearths, the clay structured hearths could be built for specific purposes.

If we treat it as a starting point the question which appears is: What such structures could have been made for?

To answer the question the author started of making a list of conclusions made on a basis of zooarchaeological, archaeobotanical and petrographical analyses available at that point:

- In the fireplaces above the clay hearths wood of a Cork Oak (*quercus suber*) was used as well as of some fruit trees (Karkanas, et al., 2004).
- In one of the clay hearths there were found starches characteristic of grass seeds (Karkanas, et al., 2004);
- In the hollow within the clay hearths no large pieces of bones were found. There were, however, numerous small fragments of bones.
- The cross–section of the clay hearths is of one hue, only the outer layer is brighter because of large amounts of ash gathered within the pores of the clay hearths.
- The clay hearths are located horizontally under a rock overhang in the vicinity of the cave. The closer to the cave the more clay hearths there are.
- The clay hearths have frequently been made one on top of the other.
- The clay hearths are in the same layer as regular fireplaces which are not above clay hearths but which seem to be made at the same time as fireplaces made directly above these structures.

The monograph of the site (Koumouzelis, Kozłowski, Stiner, 2010) lets the author add other observations.

- No phytoliths were found in samples of ashes from above clay hearth in contrary to other samples of the same layers (Albert, 2010).
- There were almost no charcoals remaining above clay hearths, although the ashes were mostly wood ashes. Wood was probably the major fuel used in the site (Ntinou, 2010).
- The distribution of the taxa identified on a basis on wood charcoals did not differ between flat hearts and clay hearths (Ntinou, 2010).

- In clay hearths mostly wood of *Acer* sp., *Prunus* sp., *Quercus* sp. was used (Ntinou, 2010).

The aim

While the project of experiments started in 2005 and lasted for 3 years aimed to answer the question of possible ways of using clay hearths in Upper Palaeolithic. While running the project before answering the question of using the structures the author should answer the question of ways of making and firing them. So while at first we limited ourselves only to testing various possibilities which are offered by burning fires over this type of structure, in order to test possible ways of using the clay hearths, during later stages of the project the focus shifted to the number of firing episodes and different ways of carrying them out and taking, if possible, measurements of temperature of the clay and the fire paying less attention to the use of the clay hearths for specific purposes.

The main purpose became to reconstruct the whole technological process of making and firing such structures and on the basis of such reconstruction to suggest few hypotheses about possible ways of using such clay structures.

For each of those stages certain questions have been raised, some of the crucial ones are the following:

- Were the clay hearths burned when dry or when still wet?
- Were these forms burned intentionally before they were properly used or whether their burning was a consequence of using them?
- The ash layer present above each of the clay hearths might point to the fact that their use involved making fire above them –was that really the case?
- Were they designed to be used only once or many times?
- Do the clay hearths change the properties of the whole fireplace, e.g.: is the temperature higher?
- Does the fireplace maintain a constant temperature for a longer period of time?
- Were there any certain activities that might have been performed only in a fireplace that has an underlying clay hearth?

The description

The project consisted of four series of experiments. A series involved many individual experiments which often

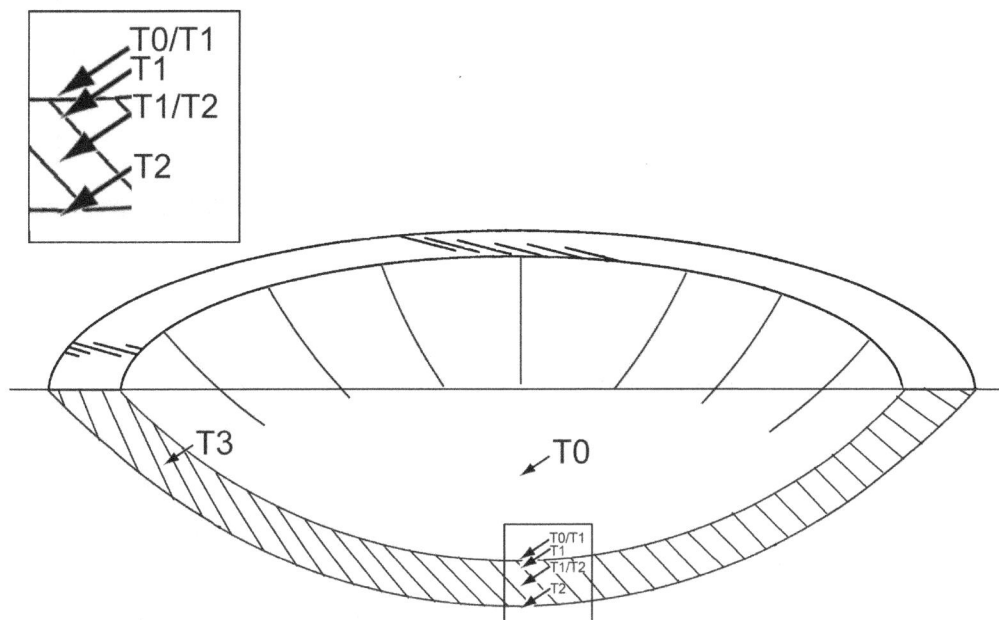

Fig. 2.1 Distribution of measurement points.

were logically connected forming small sequences, defined as cycles. First series of experiments took place in Poland and Germany. As these were the first experiments the author was focused on checking some possibilities of using clay hearts and establishing which factors can influence the result of experiment. The second series of experiments was made in Greece next to Klissoura site. The experiments were focused on comparing the properties of the clay from Klissoura Gorge. Results achieved with a different type of clay varied from those achieved with Klissoura clay. While the second series of experiment the problem of oxidizing and reducing the clay appeared. It became clear that the next step should consist of checking the temperature of the clay while firing the structures. The third and fourth series of experiments which took place in Romania and in Greece were focused on measuring the temperature of the clay structure while changing certain conditions.

During the project 34 reconstructions of the clay hearths have been made, 21 of which were produced in Greece in the very vicinity of the cave.

Each series of experiments is marked with a Roman number and the first letter of the name of the location where the experiments were performed. And so individual series are recorded using the following abbreviations: IP, IIK, IIIR, IVK, where P–means Poland, K–Klissoura and R–Romania.

Clay forms built and used during a specific series of experiments were assigned a successive Arabic numeral, marked "p" before the number, and name of the series after the number. Additionally, each successive firing of a given clay form was assigned a number. Consequently, in the description of the experiments will come across coded

names such as e.g.: III firing p2KIV, which denotes third firing of a second clay form from the fourth (last) series of experiments.

This system was adopted to make it easier after the experiments have been completed to compare freely and discuss individual experiments avoiding confusion as far as possible.

Methodology

A single experiment consisted first of building an experimental clay hearth which started of mixing the clay with a small amount of water enough for the clay to become plastic. The next step was moulding the clay into clay forms. This was done in two ways.

- The first method was by moulding 2–3cm thick small and flat rounds of clay and sticking them onto the cleaned surface of the ground to form a large and flat, lightly basin–like form.
- The second method was by moulding the entire batch of clay to be made into a clay hearth into a ball, occasionally flattened which was next placed at the centre of the hollow and pummelled into the required shape with a fist. The clay flattened by battering forms a circular form having a diameter dependent on the amount of clay used to make the ball.

During the third and fourth series of experiments up to 6 devices for measuring temperature were used –IT–AA1–K/2/SO–d3–L500–Lp1.5 (thermocouples) and one TES–1307 device. This made it possible to record the temperature of the fire and of the clay in several places in the clay hearth simultaneously.

In each ready clay–lined structure temperature sensors were installed at several different points; this was done by making ducts made in the clay to insert the tip of thermocouples at specific locations. The duct had a diameter of ca. 5mm to accommodate the tip of the sensor which had a diameter of 4.5mm. If the firing process was to follow immediately after the hollow form had been lined with clay the thermocouple was installed in the duct right away. If the form was left to dry, straws were placed within the ducts to keep their diameter from changing.

For all experiments a uniform scheme of distribution of the measuring points was adopted to make easier subsequent comparison of temperature diagrams (fig.2.1). The scheme was as follows:

$T0$– temperature readout of the fire,

$T0/T1$– temperature readout measured by touching the tip of the sensor to the surface of the clay hearth,

$T1$– readout made immediately under the surface of the clay–typically at 0.5–1cm below the surface, by introducing the thermocouple into a duct,

$T1/T2$– readout of temperature of the clay midway in the cross–section of the clay hearth,

$T2$– readout of temperature of the clay underneath the clay hearth.

$T3$– readout of temperature of the clay outside the centre of the clay hearth–by its rim.

The obtained structure was fired right after it was made–when wet–or after the clay had dried, by making a fire over the clay hearth. Another method was by filling it with embers taken from a separate fire burning nearby.

The firing process was carried out in two ways. The fire was made over the clay form, or embers from a fire made next to the form were piled over the clay form. Depending on the adopted principle the first method of firing, defined as 'direct firing' (i.e. firing with fire rather than just the embers) could be of a long (5–7 hours) or short (2–3 hours) duration. Once the firing process was over the embers were either left within the experimental clay hearth until they burnt out or removed, swept out together with the ash which had collected to clean the clay hearth.

The second method of firing was 'firing with embers'. The embers were piled over the experimental clay hearth and successively replenished during firing. Eventually, on most occasions the embers were left within the clay form until they burnt out. The aim of the second method of firing was only to heat the clay form.

During the firing process the temperature was measured every fifteen minutes. Each form was fired once or several times depending on the assumptions of the experiment, each time taking measurements of the temperature of the fire and of the clay within the clay hearth.

CHAPTER 3

FIRST SERIES OF EXPERIMENTS

The aim and methodology

The first series of experiments was conducted in 2005 in Poland and Germany. As a part of this series of experiments the planned experiments were divided into three cycles. Each cycle involved making two clay hearths. The experiments were focused on the reconstruction of the possible ways of using concave clay structures without putting much attention to the process of making, drying and firing the clay.

Making a list of possible ways of using such forms was the first step of the project. The main attention was put on testing the hypothesis concerning roasting seeds of wild grasses (Pawlikowski, et al., 2000). Testing the hypothesis was focused rather on the possible ways of roasting food by using clay structures that reconstructing process of roasting certain species of seeds. Apart from seeds of grasses other seeds and nuts were used as well. Next points were connected with testing the possibility of boiling water or roasting meat and fruits.

The description

The first cycle

This cycle involved using local glacial clay for making two clay structures. For this reason experiments were conducted in NE Poland in the postglacial region with an easy access to the clay residues.

The first form (p1PI) was left for two weeks before setting a fire. At this time clay had become dry. The experiment aimed at roasting seeds and pods of pea by putting them on the bottom of the structure and covering by embers. After the embers dyed out within 4 hours all the seeds and pods were taken out with the ashes. Out of 200 pea seeds 71% did not show any changes in colour, 18% were roasted, 11% were burned. Out of 40 pea pods all seeds were roasted.

The second clay structure (p2PI) was made of local clay as well. The form had 50cm in diameter and was 12cm deep. It was fired when still wet and the firing process lasted 4–5 hours after which the fire was left to die out. Two days latter the ashes were taken out and a direct fire was made inside the structure again. After the clay was heated embers were taken out and the clay structure was cleaned. The ears of wild grass (*Dactylis glomerata L.*) were put inside the structure. Half of them were covered by embers and half was left at the hot clay without covering. Ten minutes latter embers were taken out. The

ears and seeds which had contact with embers were mostly fired. The rest showed no changes in colour.

The third firing episode was conducted to test if the results of roasting pea seeds would change if the clay structures were heated before. The pea seeds were put inside the heated clay structure and covered by embers. Almost all the seeds burned because of the high temperature.

Apart from pea seeds there were also walnuts in the shell put under the embers. They burned as well after few minutes. Only the walnuts put at the heated clay without covering them by embers were taken out roasted and changed the flavor.

While taking photos of the clay structures, after all the experiments, the author realized that during firing the part of the clay which was in contact with the ground took on a black and dark brown hue. Inside the clay was light beige and red in hue. The clay hearths in cross section became bi–coloured–red on the top, black in the bottom.

The second cycle

The second cycle of experiment was run in The Centre of Experimental Archaeology Museumsdorf Duppel in Berlin. Two clay structures were made of fat ceramic clay obtained from a pottery–maker. The first of them (p3PI) was 37cm in diameter.

The first experiment aimed at testing if making fire inside a wet structure would have an influence on roasting seeds. This time rye seeds were used for roasting.

Because of firing, while being still wet, the clay started cracking and flaking. After firing the new layer of clay was put on the top of the cracked structure. A fire was made inside the structure again. After heating the structure, the embers were taken out of the structure and seeds were put there instead. Half of the seeds was covered by embers, the rest was left on the hot clay without covering. During the experiment the seeds which were covered by embers became bigger while heated, some of them were burned. The seed which were left without covering showed not changes in colour and size. The wet clay did not manage to heat into the temperature which would enable to roast seeds.

The second clay structure (p4PI) was 45cm in diameter and was made of the same fat ceramic clay as p3PI. The experiment was designed to test a hypothesis of boiling water inside a heated clay structure. Because of the bad weather conditions the clay structure was also fired when still wet. After 3 hours of firing all the embers were taken out and a structure was cleaned of the ashes. While still hot it was filled with water. Two stones heated in the fire before were put inside the water. The water became hot but before boiling it sank in the clay.

In the result the author started considering what does a clay structure change in the conditions of a fireplace. The clay which was used in the experiments was cracking while firing it and a process of heating was very long. The results obtained after experiments were not similar at all to the clay structures found at Klissoura site.

The third cycle

The last cycle of experiments was run in Southern Poland. The first clay structure (p5PI) was made of a clay extracted from between the limestone. The clay was reddish and had lots of little pieces of limestone inside. In comparison with all the other clays used in this series of experiment it was the most similar to the one which had been used at Klissoura site. The clay structure made of this clay was 48cm in diameter and was almost flat. It was fired after 8 days of drying in the sun. When the fire was dying apples were put inside the embers. They were baked very fast but it is hard to establish if the clay structure accelerated the process e.g. by raising the temperature of the fire. Some apples were put on the heated clay and they were baked as well.

After firing the clay structure became red–brown from the inside but black from the outside.

The next structure (p6PI) was made of sandy clay found in a gorge nearby. A structure which was made of it was 48cm in diameter and was slightly deeper than the previous one. A fire was set after 8 days of drying. After few hours of heating all the embers were taken out and the structure was filled by 1,5l of water. In 15 minutes all the water evaporated or sank in the clay and did not boil. The clay became plastic again.

The results

On the basis of the conducted experiments and 6 reconstructions of clay structures the following conclusions were made.

- Firing a wet structure causes its cracking.
- Drying a structure in the sun causes its cracking.
- A process of heating the clay differs depending on the weather conditions and the clay's conditions.
- The structure after firing becomes bicoloured–red from the top and black from bottom what was not observed in any of the structures found at Klissoura site.
- Repeated firing of the clay structure (p2PI) causes an increase of the temperature.
- In amount of 5 different clays used during the first series of experiments only the one coming from Southern Poland shows some similarities to the *terra rosa* clays and did not crack on sun while drying.
- It was possible to roast seeds or nuts on a heated clay without covering them by embers only when the structure was heated for the second or the third time. While heated for the first time the clay did not obtain a temperature which would enable one to roast seeds.
- The experiments testing the possibility of boiling the water failed. The clay was not fired yet and was still able to become plastic again (the temperature did not overcome 300°C).

After the first series of experiments the author realized that the reconstruction of possible the ways of using the structures is impossible without focusing on the whole process of making, drying and firing of the structures.

The experiments revealed that burning clay in the ground in contemporary conditions creates a reducing atmosphere in the inner part of the structure. For this reason the part of clay that touched the ground acquires a black hue after the burning process. No such colour was present in the discovered Aurignacian clay hearths. The main subject matter of following series of experiments focused on the problem of achieving an oxidising atmosphere in both the inner and the outer side of clay hearths. For this reason the second stage of the project which was started in the spring of 2006 put a special emphasis on the burning technique of the clay hearths.

CHAPTER 4

SECOND SERIES OF EXPERIMENTS

The second series of experiments was completed in June 2006 in a rock shelter with an area of ca. 15 sq m lying several score meters from the site Klissoura Cave 1. The shelter is found, like the Cave no. 1, on the same SW slope of Klissoura Gorge.

Experiments were planned in order to investigate the properties of clays used for making the clay hearths during the early Upper Palaeolithic. Taken into consideration were not only plasticity of *terra rosa* clays and their organic content but, above all, their thermic properties.

The experiments involved the building of a clay form directly on the ground or over a layer of ashes, to compare permeability of the ground and access of oxygen to the clay, depending on variable factors. Some of the clay forms were allowed to dry before being fired, others were fired when still wet to see whether wet–firing alters the thermic properties of the clay and whether the clay heats equally rapidly in these conditions and does not become fissured while being fired. Some forms were fired several times to test the impact of repeated firing on the extent of oxidation of the clay and change in colour. Finally, a part of the forms were fired by building a fire over them while some where only covered with hot embers to test the differences resulting from either firing scenario.

Two cycles of experiments were planned, the first of which was making three forms and firing them when dry, twice or three times. The first cycle included forms p1KII, p2KII and p3KII. The fact that the first of these clay structures were built of clay originating from two different locations made it possible to observe the behaviour of clay taken from different deposits. Additionally, one of the forms (p1KII) was built directly on the ground, the second (p2KII), over ashes and embers, the third (p3KII) was to be fired on both sides by being exposed simultaneously to an open fire from below and from the top (fig.4.1).

The second cycle was to test two clay forms which were to be fired when still wet. One of these forms was to be fired with an open fire built over it (p4KII), the second, by burying under a layer of embers (p5KII). Ultimately the author decided to additionally repeat the experiment with firing a wet form using embers and another form– p6KII–was made (fig.4.2). The aim of this series of experiments was to observe the clay during and after firing while still wet and comparing the degree of firing of clay subjected directly to fire or heated with embers.

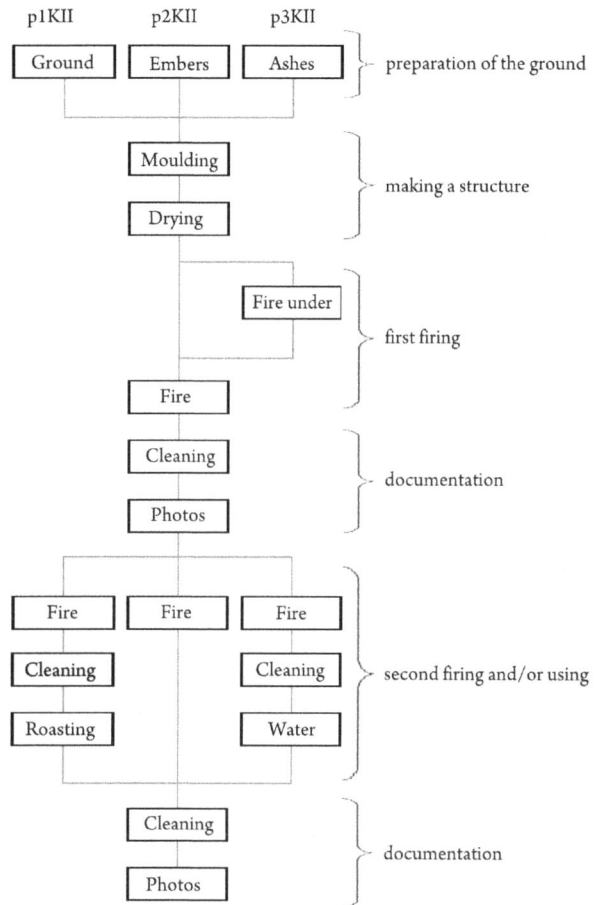

Fig. 4.1 Scheme of the first cycle of experiments including p1KII, p2KII and p3KII.

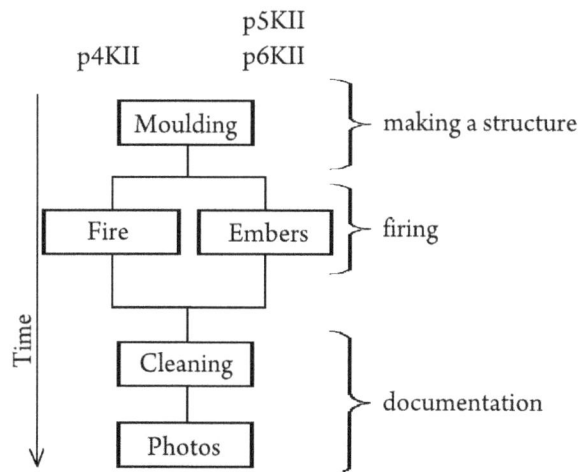

Fig. 4.2 Scheme of the second cycle of experiments including p4KII, p5KII and p6KII.

Methods

Two types of clay were used in making the clay forms. One deposit was identified about 1km to the west of Cave Klissoura in the Berbadiotis river gorge. The gorge at this point expands to a flat plain which stretches to the sea. The clay occurred in the wall of the dry river bed. It was light beige in colour, with observable white calcite precipitates. The clay was substantially dehydrated and fossilised and could be extracted only with a pick and a shovel. In the present report this material is referred to as "no. 1 clay". The second clay deposit used in the experiments lies some 1–1.5 km to the east, moving up the river valley towards the village of Prosimni. The outcrop was in the slope of the valley some 5 metres above the valley bottom. This clay was darker in colour as compared to no. 1 clay and had no evident traces of calcination. On the surface of the deposit the clay was friable but at the depth of some 15cm it was moist which made it easier to extract. In the discussion below it is referred to as "no. 2 clay".

During experiments thermocouples needed to measure the temperature of the fire were not available. The highest temperature obtained in the fires during firing could be estimated only after firing was over by examining the colour of animal bones which had been thrown into the fire.

After each firing episode samples of clay were taken from the clay forms. This was easier if the form had cracked during firing; otherwise, the author either decided to break off a fragment of the clay or only to photograph the bottom part of the clay form.

P1KII

Originally p1KII had the diameter of 42x41cm and a depth of 4cm. It was built of no. 1 clay and placed right next to the entrance to the rock shelter where it was exposed to sunlight for several hours each day.

Plans were made to fire this form three times and to examine the change in the colour of the clay in cross-section after each firing (fig.4.1). During the second and third firing plans were made also to roast nuts and meat over the heated clay.

The clay was left to dry for 2 days before the first firing which was of three hours' duration. After this time no more fuel was added to the fire and it was allowed to go out. The next day the form was swept clean of the ashes. After firing the clay had become fissured in some places. On the inside it had turned red–grey–black, on the outside it was red at centre and black on the sides.

The next firing was carried out the same day. The fire burnt over the form for about 3 hours. After this time all the embers were swept out from the form and hazelnuts placed onto the heated clay. Once they were in contact with the hot clay the nuts started to burn and had to be turned over. The process of roasting which lasted some

5–10 minutes resulted in the roasting of the nuts. After this treatment the form was left to cool.

After the second firing no new cracks in the clay appeared but fissures which had developed earlier had grown wider so that ashes and air could penetrate deeper into the clay. Perhaps, fissuring of the clay forms was the cause of partial oxidation of the entire form which on the outside had turned non–uniform dark brown in colour.

The aim of the third firing was to heat the form as fast as possible and lasted only 1.5 hours. After this time the embers and burning wood were removed and the clay was cleaned of the ashes. Due to high temperature it was easiest to remove the ashes by blowing at them. Removing ashes with twigs, bunches of grass or with a paintbrush was difficult as these materials began to burn and the clay turned white when minute particles of ash were rubbed into the pores in the clay. After the ashes had been removed, thin strips of raw beef were placed onto the heated clay. The aim of the experiment was testing whether it is possible to roast meat directly over heated clay. During roasting the meat had to be turned. It became roasted after about 10–15 minutes.

After three firing episodes the clay had turned red over its entire surface, both on the inside and on the outside. Despite the fact that the clay had already cracked when drying and later, during the first firing, fragments which had not become fissured had been fired very hard forming a compact mass. In order to take a clay sample the form had to be broken with a stone to break off a fragment of the clay.

P2KII

Form p2KII was built at the very end of the shelter, by the wall, which during the summer always remains in the shade. Its material was no. 2 clay. The form had a diameter of 43x44cm and a depth of 5cm. It was set over a layer of embers and other remains of an earlier open fire made on this spot. The aim of the experiment was to test the behaviour of clay built into a form not directly over the ground but over a less compacted substrate expected to ensuring better oxygen access (fig.4.1).

Form p2KII was exposed to fire three days after it was made. The first firing lasted 3 hours. After this time the embers were left to go out. During the firing animal bones were thrown into the fire. They burnt to a non–uniform colour and in some places had turned white, suggesting that the temperature of the fire had exceeded 700°C (Walker and Miller, 2005; Walker, Miller and Richman, 2008). Most of them were grey in colour indicating a temperature of 500–700°C.

After the firing the clay on the inside was not uniform in colour. Inside, at bottom, it had turned black, the rest had become red and red–brown. The clay sample taken after the first firing and placed in water reverted entirely to its original state and disintegrated in the water in a manner analogous to samples taken from prehistoric clay hearths from Klissoura.

On its underside the entire form had turned red. Also adhering to the clay at bottom were some pieces of charcoal over which the clay had been made. In cross–section the clay was a uniform red colour except for its centre where the break was two–coloured: black at top and red at bottom (Pl.1.3). The dark colour appeared on the break in this place at the depth of around 5mm. Its may have been caused by lack of access of oxygen to the clay in the central area of the form.

The second firing lasted three hours. The clay at bottom remained red but here and there a darker black–dark brown colour had appeared. On the underside, it was covered with ashes which had penetrated into the pores in the external layer of the clay. The clay itself had remained red. After being placed in water the clay did not fully revert to its original state.

P3KII

This form was of no. 2 clay and had a diameter of 48x49cm and a depth of 11cm. The clay was left to dry in the shade for three days. After this time it was lifted from the ground. Despite that fact that it had not been fired the clay had not fissured and could be taken out whole and turned upside down for photographic documentation.

Before the form was placed again in the ground a fire was made at bottom of the hollow. Next, the form was placed on top of the burning fire. Because of the fire the form no longer fit well inside the hollow from which it had been lifted; it rested slightly at an angle and protruded over the surface of the ground. Note, that this form was exceptionally deep and had a substantial diameter which could have the cause of this difficulty. The aim of this experiment was to test the appearance of clay exposed to an open fire on both its sides during firing (from below and from the top) (fig.4.1).

A second fire was built on top of the form which had been placed over a fire made inside the hollow. The firing lasted for some 3 hours, although the fire burning below the form soon went out, first, because it had been smothered by the overlying form, second, because it could not be fed by adding more fuel. The fire on top of the form burnt much longer. After three hours the embers were left inside the form to burn themselves out.

After the form was removed from the ground the next day it was found that at the point of contact of the clay with the fire from below the clay had turned deep red whereas outside this area the clay on the outer face was dark brown and black in colour. The parts next to the rim had not become fired because, as was mentioned earlier, the form was quite deep and the fire did not reach as far as the rim of the clay form. On the inside the clay had turned the same range of colours as on the outside–it was red at bottom. This place was surrounded by a few centimetre's zone of black colour. Next to the rim, the clay had not

changed colour because it had not been fired at all. During firing animal bones were thrown into the fire. They had burnt to a grey colour indicating that the temperature of the fire did not exceed 700°C. (Walker, Miller, Richman, 2008).

The aim of the second firing was to see to what extent it is possible to boil water and keep it inside a form heated previously by burning a fire over it.

During the second firing which lasted three hours the fire was made only inside the form. After three hours the burning wood, embers and ashes were removed and water was poured into the still hot form. Due to substantial degree of fissuring the water did not stay for long inside the form–it soon was absorbed by the clay, leaked out or partly evaporated. The clay form itself, as a result of the second firing and filling with water, became considerably fissured. The aim of the experiment (to use it for boiling water) had not been achieved because the form was excessively fissured.

After the second firing the clay had not changed colour except for a zone near the rim which had been fired and turned red. The clay on the outer face was non–uniform red–black.

P4KII

This form was made at the entrance to the rock shelter right next to form p1KII. Its material was no. 1 clay. The finished structure had a diameter of 39x38cm and a depth of 4.5cm. Immediately after it was made the form was fired.

The aim of the first firing was to test the behaviour of *terra rosa* clay when fired wet (fig.4.2). The firing lasted 3 hours. After firing was over the embers where pushed to the side and raw and unripe almonds with a green shell were placed on the hot clay and buried with embers and ashes. After the embers had gone out it was found that the almonds had burnt completely. During firing the clay did not crack and the structure survived entire. To take samples and examine its cross–section the form was broken in half. The clay over the entire surface had turned beige.

The aim of the second firing was to check whether the colour of the clay would not change if it was exposed once again to a high temperature. With this in mind another fire was made over the form and sustained for three hours. While the fire was burning some of the embers were transferred in stages to form p5KII which was being fired at this time by being spread over with embers. At the end of the firing all the embers were taken out of the form and it was swept clean of ashes, and as a next step, when it had cooled to some extent, hazelnuts were placed on its surface. The nuts roasted much more poorly in comparison to nuts subjected to a similar heat treatment inside form p1KII. The different result presumably was caused by the fact that the form had had time to cool slightly before nuts were placed inside it.

The form was exposed once more to high temperature, for around half an hour, when it was filled with embers taken from over form p1KII, when it was cleared after the end of the third firing.

After all the firing episodes the clay had turned non–uniform dark brown–red. On the surface it was more beige in colour, on the underside, darker, passing to dark brown. Inside the ceramic mass there were black traces of charred organic matter.

P5KII

The material of this form was no. 1 clay. Before being caked over with clay the entire hollow was coated with a layer of ashes. The form had a diameter of 32cm and a depth of 2.5cm. It was fired without being allowed to dry. The form was to be fired filling with the greatest possible amount of embers without an open fire made over it.

The aim of this experiment was to see whether firing with embers, rather than with an open fire, would alter the thermic properties of the clay, cause oxidisation or reduction of iron compounds in the clay, and finally, to test the behaviour of wet clay exposed to high temperature (fig.4.2).

The first firing lasted 6 hours. During this entire time embers were successively replenished from fires which were being burnt half a metre away over forms p1KII and p4KII. After this time the embers were pushed aside and hazelnuts placed at centre and roasted within 5–10 minutes. This was done to test the extent to which the clay had become heated. After the hazelnuts were removed a few raw potatoes were placed at bottom of the form, covered with a large quantity of embers and left until they died down. The next day the ashes were raked up but all the potatoes had burnt completely, some without a trace indicating that the temperature of the embers and the clay itself had continued to be relatively high for a long time.

After the firing the clay on its inner side turned black in places, on the outside, it became red. When the form was lifted from the ground a fragment of its rim broke which made it possible to examine its cross–section. In some places in the break two layers could be observed: on top this was a very slender black layer, at bottom the clay was red. In addition, around the empty spaces left by burnt our organic matter the clay had turned black; in some places charred but not burnt out organic matter was visible. Placed in water the clay reverted to its original state.

The second firing also involved spreading the form with embers taken from a nearby fire. This firing lasted 2 hours. Next, the embers around the form were pushed to the side and shelled almonds placed onto the clay and roasted fairly soon. The form was lifted, swept clean of embers and ashes, dried and photographed.

The colour of the clay during the second firing had not changed; it remained red–beige over the entire cross–section. Within the clay black spaces around the burnt out particles of organic matter were still visible and in places, charred organic matter itself (Pl.1.2). The slender black layer observed on the surface of the clay after the first firing had become oxidised. Placed in water the clay reverted fully to its original state.

P6KII

The material of this form was no. 1 clay. The structure was made by plastering with clay the sides of a hollow dug in the ground. The diameter of the form was 35cm.

The aim this time was to see whether the Palaeolithic clay forms were exposed only to a limited extent to high temperature by being spread over with embers (fig.4.2).

As part of this experiment a wet form was filled with embers for about 3 hours. Whereas during an earlier experiment made with form p5KII the embers had covered almost the entire form during this particular experiment the embers were placed only at the bottom of the clay form leaving its rim during firing free from the embers. After three hours the embers were raked aside and nuts placed on the clay and roasted although this took more time than in case of nuts being roasted at the same time using form p5KII.

After the first firing the inside and underside of the form continued to be wet and had not become fired. Therefore it was decided to fire it a second time. That same day another fire was made over the form and burned for a short time but insufficient amount of wood available at that time made it impossible to build a fire with a higher temperature.

After this firing was over it was found that the clay had not become fired and that the ceramic mass still contained fragments of unburnt organic matter in the form of fragments of grasses and other plants. Despite being exposed to temperature the clay had not lost its plasticity and placed in water reverted to its original state.

Experiment results

The results from this series of experiments clearly demonstrated how the difference between *terra rosa* clay and post–glacial clays known from the area of the European Lowland which had come under glaciations during the Pleistocene.

1. *Terra rosa* clays differ by having very low shrinkage properties as compared to glacial clays; this prevents them from contracting and fissuring during the process of drying. Thanks to this property *terra rosa* clays need very little or no artificial additives (i.e. temper). It performs also well when dried out in open sunlight–it does not crack and even if it does then only to a limited extent and this fissuring does not cause the destruction or disintegration of the whole form. Forms which the author

moulded during the experiments were allowed to dry in the sun in a temperature of around 40°C. On the other hand, the process of drying vessels made of glacial clays is much more complicated. The clay has to dry in the shade, in a well aired place with the right humidity and even then many vessels put out to dry crack and are not suitable for firing.

2. After drying these forms could be taken out of the ground entire, they did not disintegrate or break into fragments. Only during attempts to turn the form upside down, in some (p1KII and p3KII) fragments of the rim broke off. Forms built of post–glacial clay could not be lifted from the ground because they cracked at every attempt made to move them.

3. Even if fired without being allowed to dry, the forms usually do not crack. Fissures, if they do appear, do not cause a full disintegration of the basin–like form.

4. *Terra rosa* clay heats rapidly during firing and retains the heat over a long time. The level to which it became heated was is much higher than in earlier experiments made using glacial clays. This makes it possible to use the heated clay after it has been cleared of embers and swept clean, for roasting meat, something which was not possible or did not work well with forms tested during earlier experiments. The rapid heating could be connected to the type of surface on which the forms were built. Experiments conducted in Poland showed that the clay does not become heated too quickly, possibly because the forms were moulded in the ground with a much higher moisture level. Clay deposits found in the rock shelter, similarly as those found in front of Cave 1 at Klissoura, were quite friable and dry. Because of this, the clay during firing did not have to release a great amount of heat to the surrounding soil and became heated more quickly.

5. *Terra rosa* clay underwent the same processes of oxidation and reduction as was observed after the first firing of the form p1KII. During firing the clay turned red on the inside while on the outside it became black–dark brown in colour.

6. With each consecutive firing episode the dark layer on the underside of the form became smaller but it was very difficult to achieve an entirely red colour of the clay; this is because the person in charge of the firing could not regulate inflow of oxygen to all the places in the form. Because of this, it often happens that the clay does not have a uniform colour, with some darker or black places (I firing p3KII).

7. The building of a form directly over ashes or over the remains of an earlier fire–charcoal and ash–contributed to an increased inflow of oxygen from below; this caused the clay to turn red also on the underside of the form.

8. A uniform red cross–section was obtained after the forms had been fired without being allowed to dry. They were fired not by an open fire built over them but by piling them with hot embers. The duration of firing necessary when using this method (firing with embers) is longer. If the temperature of the embers is low or their quantity is too small the clay after firing remained unfired and wet (p6KII). The presence in the ceramic mass of particles of organic matter shows that the clay in this experiment had not been exposed to a temperature higher than 250°C.

9. Despite the fact that the firing episode p5KII lasted 6 hours and the firing episode p4KII only 3 hours, and both forms were fired in similar conditions by spreading embers over the wet form, the clay in p4KII became fired whereas, as a result of firing, the clay of p6KII developed black borders around the burnt out particles of organic matter. In p4KII there was a much smaller number of these.

10. The experiments demonstrated that in order to heat a form sufficiently to make possible e.g. heat treatment of various foodstuffs over the heated clay it was enough to fire the form for only three hours.

CHAPTER 5

THIRD SERIES OF EXPERIMENTS

Experiments made in the Centre of Experimental Archaeology in Vadastra in Romania (Kot, 2008a, 2008b) represent the third part of the project. Their aim was to reconstruct the temperature conditions of the clay hearths during firing. The crucial questions were as follows:

- How does the temperature of the clay change in different areas of the clay hearths in relation to the temperature of the fire itself?
- Are there any maximum temperatures which can be obtained during firing?
- How does it change the temperature of the clay if the clay hearths are fired while the clay is dry or wet?
- Does it change the temperature of the clay when the clay hearths are fired repeatedly?
- Does it influence the temperature of the clay if the clay hearth is situated underneath another clay structure which is being fired?

Apart from the question connected with temperature of the clay the study had a number of other aims. Earlier experiments had revealed that burning clay in the ground in contemporary conditions creates a reducing atmosphere in the inner part of the structure. As a result, the part of the clay touching the ground acquires a black hue after the burning process. No such hue was observed in the Aurignacian clay hearths (Karkanas, et al., 2004). For this reason in the new series of experiments special emphasis was put on the burning technique of the clay hearths.

The author of the experiments found it necessary also to check if during firing of an experimental clay hearth placed on clayey ground there was no similar effect of a red–burnt layer of clay directly underlying the layer of ash.

Assumptions

As part of this series of experiments the planned experiments were divided into three cycles. The first cycle involved making four clay hearths from clay brought from Klissoura. Two of these forms (p1RIII, p3RIII) were to be subjected to repeated firing. In one of the firing episodes the fire was to be extinguished by piling earth on it. Two additional clay forms (p2RIII, p4RIII) were to be modelled and fired when still wet, one of them (p4RIII) made over an already fired similar structure and buried in embers (fig.5.1).

The second cycle was to involve the making of two experimental clay hearths from local ceramic clay, fired dry (p5RIII) and wet (p6RIII) (fig.5.2).

As part of the third cycle it was decided to test if it is possible to distinguish in the cross–section the experimental clay hearth from the clayey substrate affected by the firing process, assuming that the clay hearth was made of the same clay as the one on which the fire would be made. Thus, it was decided to make the experimental hearth p7KIV of clay extracted from the substrate over which the experiments were being made. The fires were to be made inside basins left after extracting the clay (j1RIII). It was also decided to document, while the experiments were being made, the appearance of other cross–sections of the clayey substrate over which the fire was made (j2RIII, j3RIII) (fig.5.2).

Methodology

Three clay hearths were made of clay taken from the river valley in the Klissoura Gorge. This clay has specific properties. It is naturally very thin and, at the same time, very plastic. It hardly breaks even if dried in the open sun. When burnt in a temperature as low as 600°C it nevertheless becomes very hard and solid. Because of the above mentioned properties results achieved with a different type of clay may differ from those achieved using Klissoura clay.

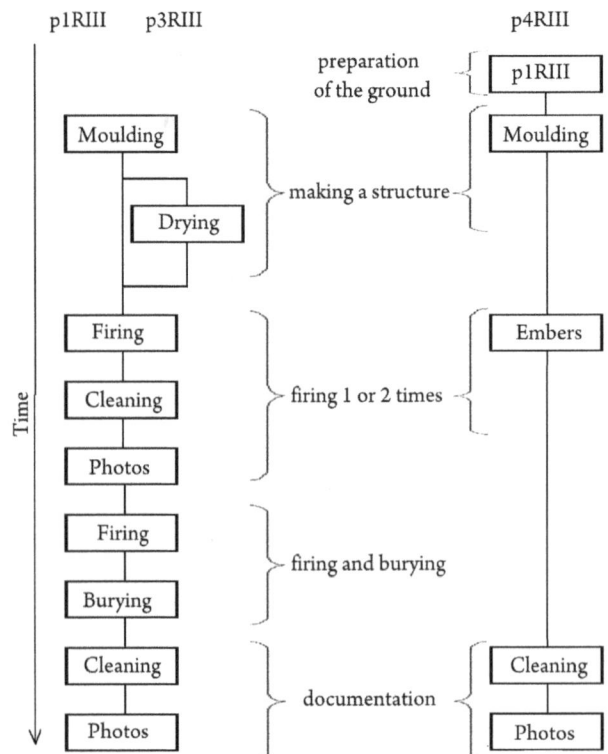

Fig. 5.1 Scheme of the first cycle of experiments including p1RIII, p3RIII and p4RIII.

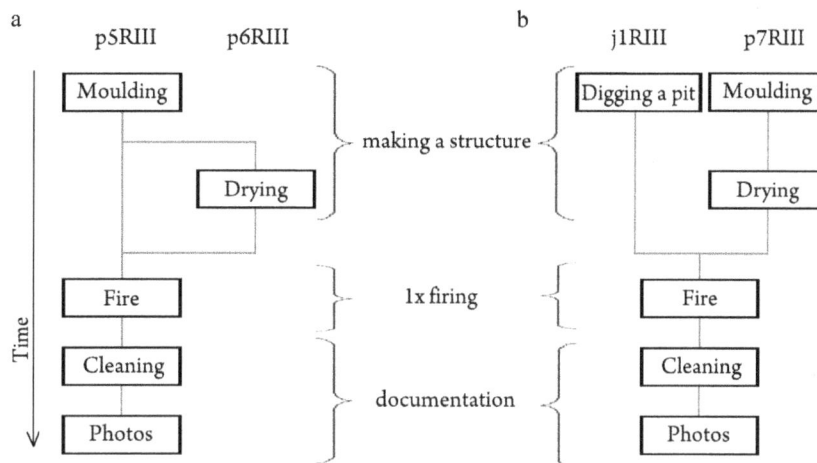

Fig. 5.2 Schemes of (a) the second cycle of experiments including p5RIII and p6RIII; (b) the third cycle of experiments including j1RIII and p7RIII.

To make some comparisons, two clay hearths were made of a local grey ceramic clay well prepared by a pottery maker and another clay–structure made of local clay extracted at the site. The firing process was carried out in two ways. The fire was made over the clay form, or embers from a fire made next to the form were piled over the clay form.

P1RIII and P4RIII

The first form (p1RIII) was fired after the clay had become dry. The first firing process lasted 7 hours. The mean temperature of the fire was 682.1°C. The temperature of the clay immediately under the surface of the experimental clay hearth (T1) was on average 173.84°C lower than the temperature of the fire itself. During the firing process the clay at bottom (T2) heated up to 271°C (fig.5.3). During firing the part of the clay in contact with the substrate took on a black and dark brown hue, similarly as the clayey substrate over which the form p1RIII had been made. On its inside the clay was light beige and red in hue.

The second firing process lasted 3.5 hours. After this time earth was piled over the fire burning inside the experimental clay hearth, all the while taking temperature sensor readouts. The embers buried under a layer of soil burnt out only after more than 10 hours. During the firing process the mean temperature of the fire was 688.64°C, the temperature under the surface of the clay at point T1 was lower, on the average, by 13.78°C. The temperature of the bottom layer of the clay hearth achieved a maximum value of 528°C (fig.5.3). During firing, the entire outer surface of the clay took on a red–beige hue. The black and black–brown hue disappeared. The inner surface developed a blue–gray hue in a layer of some 1cm.

Before starting the third firing process the form was given a new lining of clay (p4RIII). Sensors were placed according to the different scheme to measure the temperature of both experimental clay hearths. The scheme was as follows:

T0– temperature readout of the fire;
T1– readout made immediately under the surface of the clay of p4RIII;
T2– readout of temperature of the clay underneath the clay hearth p4RIII, above p1RIII;
T3– readout of temperature of the clay underneath the clay hearth p1RIII.

The aim of the experiment was to test the behaviour during the firing process of the form directly overlying the earlier hearth (a situation noted frequently at Klissoura) and to see if covering the form with a large quantity of embers and ash would bring similar results as during firing II of p1RIII and firing III of p3RIII. During firing the fire was made half a metre away from the form p4RIII, with the embers and ashes as also animal bone (used for fuel) placed over the still wet form p4RIII. The embers were topped up for five more hours, after which the fire was left to die out and measurements were taken for the next hour and a half.

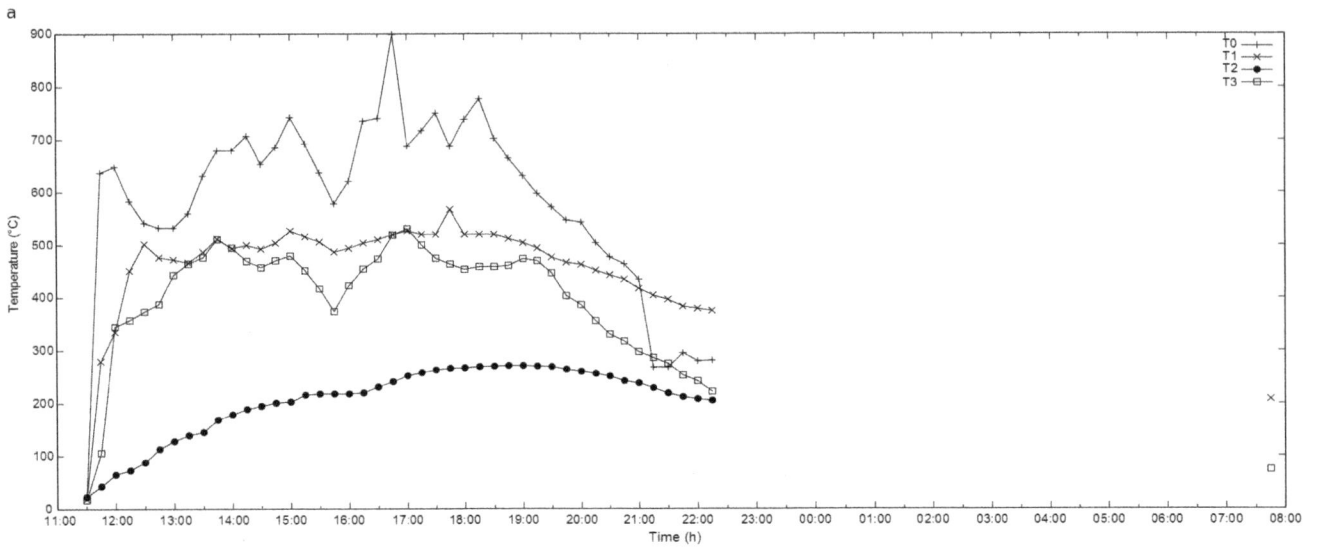

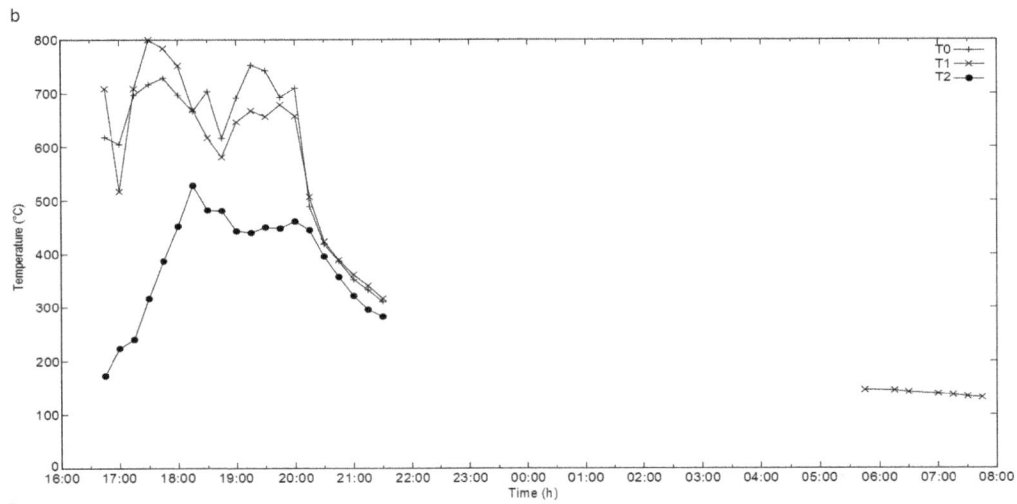

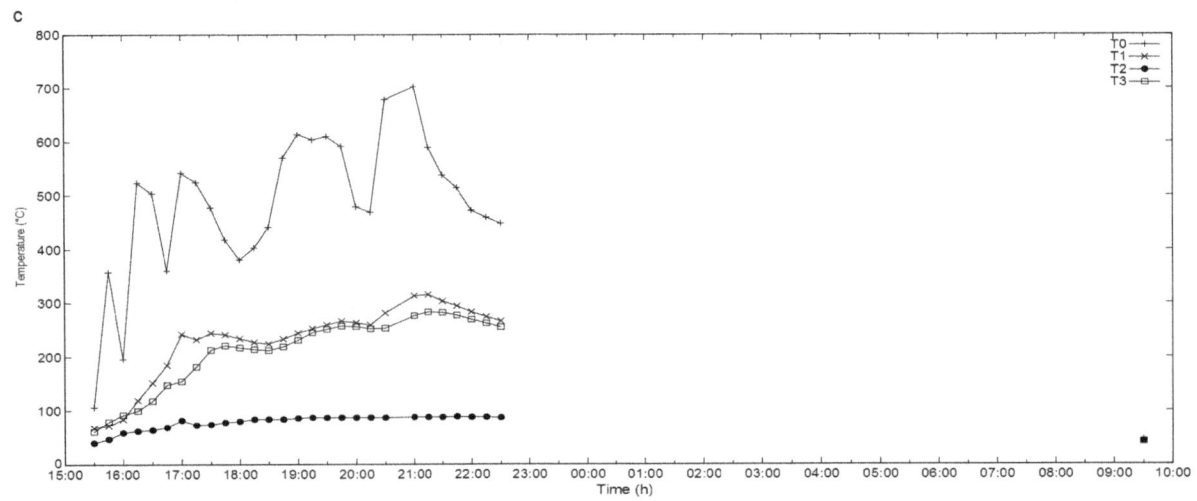

Fig. 5.3 Temperature distribution in form p1RIII during a) the first firing episode; b) the second firing episode; c) the third firing episode including temperature distribution in forms p4RIII (T0–temperature of the fire; T1–temperature just under the surface of p4RIII–not more than 5mm; T2–temperature on the bottom of the clay structure p4RIII, T3–temperature under the bottom clay structure p1RIII).

20

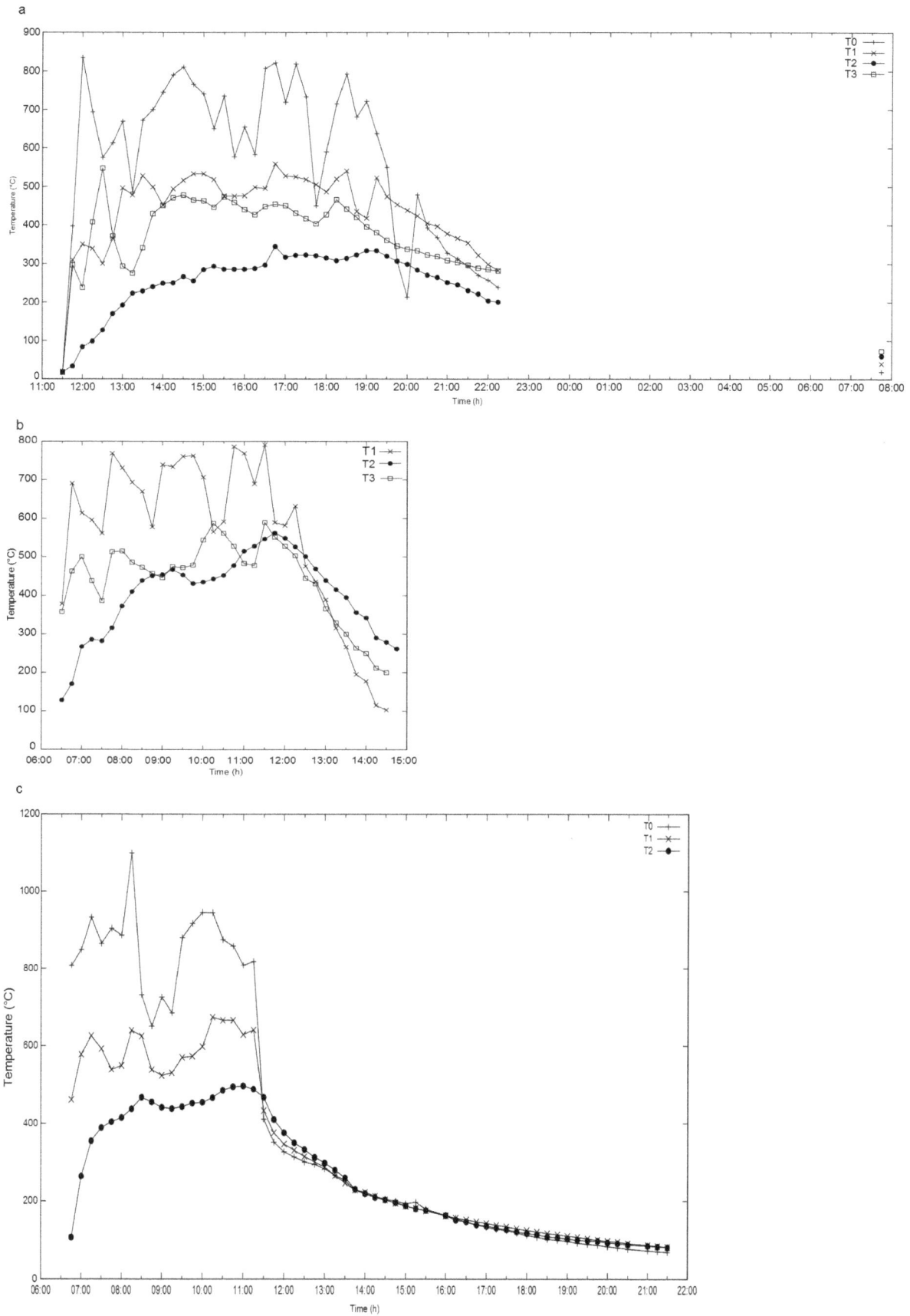

Fig. 5.4 Temperature distribution in form p3RIII during a) the first firing episode; b) second firing episode; c) third firing episode (T0–temperature of the fire; T1–temperature just under the surface–not more than 5mm; T2–temperature on the bottom of the clay structure; T3–temperature of the clay outside the centre of the clay hearth–by its rim).

21

The mean temperature of the embers was quite low, at 479.73°C. The temperature at point T1 was on average 213.51°C. The values of temperature at point T3 were very similar to those in T1, where the mean temperature of firing was 193.5°C (max. 283°C). The most stable temperature prevailed at point T2 (fig.5.3). The mean value of temperature there was 76.59°C. The maximum value of 89.1°C was noted after 6 hours of firing.

After firing, form p4RIII had turned partly red, both on the inside and on the outside, whereas the hue of the clay in p1RIII did not change, presumably because during the firing process the temperature of p1RIII did not exceed 300°C (on the surface) and 100°C (on the underside of the form).

P3RIII

Form p3RIII was moulded from clay taken from the Klissoura Gorge and fired after it had become dry by direct fire made inside it. The first firing process lasted 7 hours. The temperature of the fire was very unstable, and ranged between 450 and 835°C due to strong gusts of wind. The mean value T0 was at 655.82°C. The temperature at point T1 was on average 456.67°C (max. 558°C). After an hour of firing, the temperature on the rim of the experimental clay hearth achieved the value of 548°C after which it dropped rapidly to 275°C, and next stabilised during the third hour of firing at a fairly stable level of 400–500°C (fig.5.4). At the bottom of the clay lining the temperature was the least susceptible to varying external conditions and increased gradually during firing. During the final hour of the firing process the temperature at this point reached a maximum value of 333°C.

After firing, the underside of the experimental clay hearth touching the substrate took on a black and black–brown hue, its upper side affected by the fire–turned a red–brown hue with darker patches.

The second firing process lasted 4.5 hours and involved burning 18.2kg wood and cattle vertebrae. The temperature of the fire (T0) ranged between 550 and 800°C (fig.5). The temperature of the outer parts of the clay form depended largely on T0 but on average was lower by 257.26°C. The mean value T3 was 491.91°C. Value T2 increased steadily throughout the duration of firing. After an hour of firing a temperature of 300°C was obtained, followed by 400°C, after another 30 minutes. From this moment the rate of increase levelled off and the maximum value of 500°C was obtained after 4.5 hours of firing. After the second firing process the inner face of the experimental clay hearth took on red–beige hue all over, while the outer face partly remained black (ca. 75%) or took on a red hue (25%).

The third firing process lasted 5 hours, after which the fire was buried under a layer of earth, similarly as during firing II of p1RIII, and temperature measurements continued to be made over the next 10 hours. The temperature of the fire continued during the firing process at a very high level, with an average value of 852.05°C,

and after half an hour reached 1100°C. However, it must be noted that the measurements of T0 may not be correct because they could not be calibrated properly. The temperature at point T1 also assumed very high values, something which lends credibility to results obtained for T0. The mean temperature of firing T1 was 590.42°C and on average was lower by 261.63°C than the value of T0. The maximum value of temperature at point T1–674°C–was obtained after three and a half hours of firing (fig.5.4).

The lowest temperatures were recorded at the underside of the clay lining–at point T2. Their average value was 418.42°C. After five hours of firing the form was covered with a layer of earth which caused a very rapid drop in temperature. After the third firing the entire experimental clay hearth took on a beige–red hue, both on the outside and on the inside.

P5RIII

Form p5RIII was made of ceramic clay obtained from a local pottery–maker. This was excellently rendered lean grey clay (5Y3/1 4.1 according to the Munsell colour system).

The first firing process lasted 5 hours. The mean temperature of the fire was 791°C, with a maximum value of 936°C noted two and a half hours after lighting the fire (fig.7). The mean value of temperature at point T3 was 345.04°C (max. 608°C). The mean temperature at point T2 was 180.57°C. A maximum value (315°C) was recorded after four and a half hours of firing (fig.5.5).

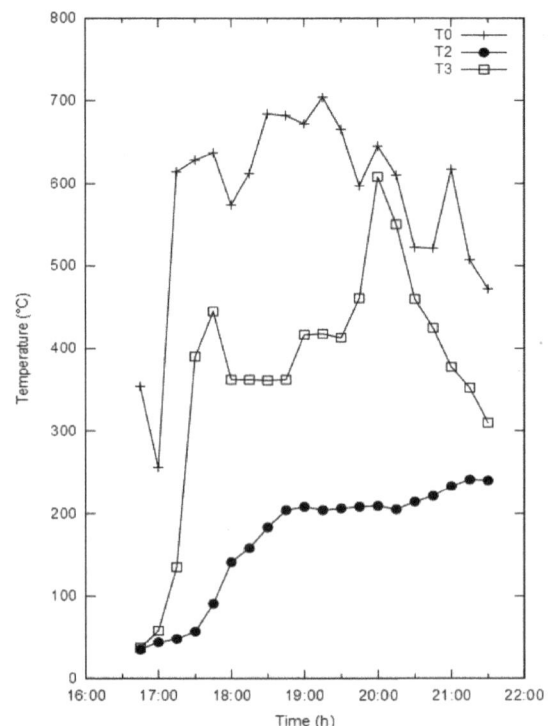

Fig. 5.5 Temperature distribution in form p5RIII during the first firing episode (T0–temperature of the fire; T2–temperature on the bottom of the clay structure; T3–temperature of the clay outside the centre of the clay hearth–by its rim).

After the firing process the clay on the inside took on a red hue on about a half of its surface, the rest became black as a result of firing. On the outside, 80% of the surface of the clay took on a red hue. Only on the rims of the form, next to the rim, it developed a brown hue. The red hue on the outer face of the form may have resulted from the fact that the form had become slightly detached from the substrate after inserting below it of a temperature sensor.

P6RIII

Form p6RIII was made of ceramic clay–the same as used to make p5RIII. It was fired when still wet and the firing process lasted 6.5 hours. A total of ca. 17kg wood was used. The fluctuation of temperature at point was T0 very high, due to atmospheric conditions, mainly windy weather. The mean temperature T0 was 624.6°C, the maximum temperature–860°C (fig.5.6). Temperatures at point T1 were lower on average than T0 by 495.67°C. A maximum value of 196.5°C was noted at this point after 11 and a half hours of firing. The mean temperature at point T3 was 210.81°C (max. 284°C). The lowest temperatures were observed at point T2. A maximum value of 79.8°C was recorded 9 hours after the start of the experiment. The mean temperature of firing was 71.88°C, the temperature increment very low, similarly as the rate of decrease. The clay did not change the hue during firing and remained blue–grey. The range of temperatures obtained at the bottom of the form, at point T4, indicates that not only the clay had not been fired, it even did not

lose all of its water since the temperature had not exceeded 100°C.

P7RIII

Form number 7 was made of local clay extracted in direct vicinity of the experimentation site. Before being made into the experimental clay hearth the clay was not rendered lean. The first firing process lasted 5 hours and used up 15.5kg wood. The temperature of the fire was relatively stable and continued at the level of 600–700°C. At point T1 the mean value of temperature during firing was 334.85°C (max. 517°C). At the bottom of the clay hearth a maximum temperature of 353°C was achieved at the time when the firing process was over (fig.5.7). The mean temperature of firing at point T2 was 194.91°C. During firing the form broke apart into a number of large fragments and it was decided to leave it without documenting the appearance of its underside/outer surface. On the inside the clay had become mottled. By the rim its hue was red, at centre–black and black–brown.

The second firing process lasted 4 hours and used up a small quantity of wood with a large proportion of animal bone, which explains the low temperature of the fire (max. 440°C). The mean temperature at point T0 was 391.95°C. Value T1 increased rapidly over the first two hours of firing until it reached the maximum level of 300°C. After this time the rate of increase dropped off. The maximum value of temperature just under the surface of clay was 347°C. The mean temperature of the bottom of the clay lining (T3) was 200.58°C (max. 273°C).

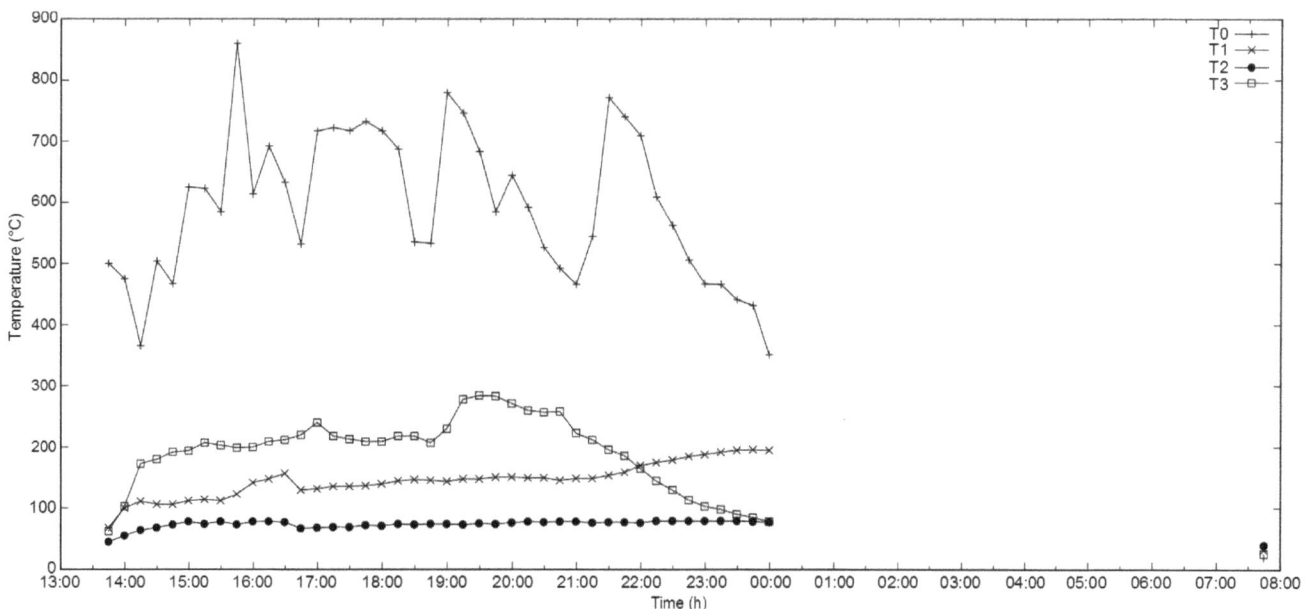

Fig. 5.6 Temperature distribution in form p6RIII during the first firing episode (T0–temperature of the fire; T1–temperature just under the surface–not more than 5mm; T2–temperature on the bottom of the clay structure; T3–temperature of the clay outside the centre of the clay hearth–by its rim).

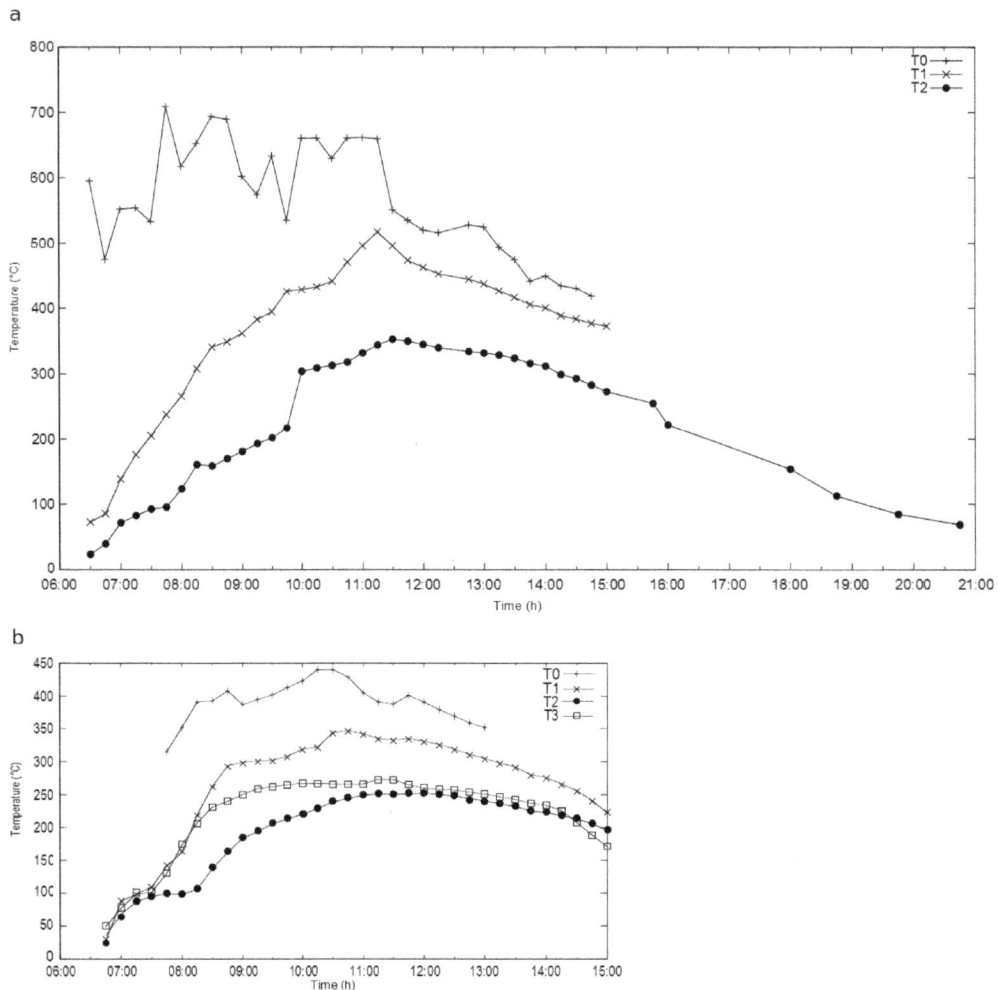

Fig. 5.7 Temperature distribution in form p7RIII during a) the first firing episode; b) the second firing episode (T0–temperature of the fire; T1–temperature under the surface–not more than 5mm; T2–temperature on the bottom of the clay structure; T3–temperature of the clay outside the centre of the clay hearth–by its rim).

Next to lining the forms with clay it was decided to make an experiment to determine whether clay forms similar in outlook may develop as a result of burning a fire over a clayey substrate. Availability of a clayey substrate in the immediate vicinity of the site where experiments made it possible to examine each time the appearance of the substrate after the removal of the clay form at the end of the experiment. Additionally, on three occasions, fires were made on a substrate cleared of plants to verify the appearance of the clay in cross–section.

Clay hollows

Observation of the section of the substrate affected by the fire (j1RIII) shows that a layer of fired and red clay was discontinuous (Pl.1.5,6). There was no clear boundary between the layer of fired and unfired clay, or at least, the layer of clay subjected to temperature and clay not affected by the heat. However, these observations were not comprehensive as the maximum values of temperature of the soil layer at the depth of around 2cm–T1 and around 4cm–T3 of 170°C and

136°C respectively, showed that the clay under the fire had not been modified by firing. Similar temperature distribution was obtained by March, Ferreri and Guez (1993, fig.1,2) in their experiments on combustion structures.

A new fire was made on the ground which during firing I of p1RIII had been under this form and which after firing took on a black hue (j2RIII). A section made through the layer of clay below the fire revealed the presence of a profile of three hues (Pl.1.4). The upper layer of clay had been fired red. The layer of clay in between became black, the clay underneath was grey–beige in hue, not modified by temperature change which did not reach to this depth. Despite the fact that the layers differed in hue there was no clear boundary between the sediment underlying the clay which had become fired and the clay itself, as is the case at Klissoura.

A section made through another pit found underneath p1RIII during firing II confirmed the earlier observations. This section was also of three hues (red

a

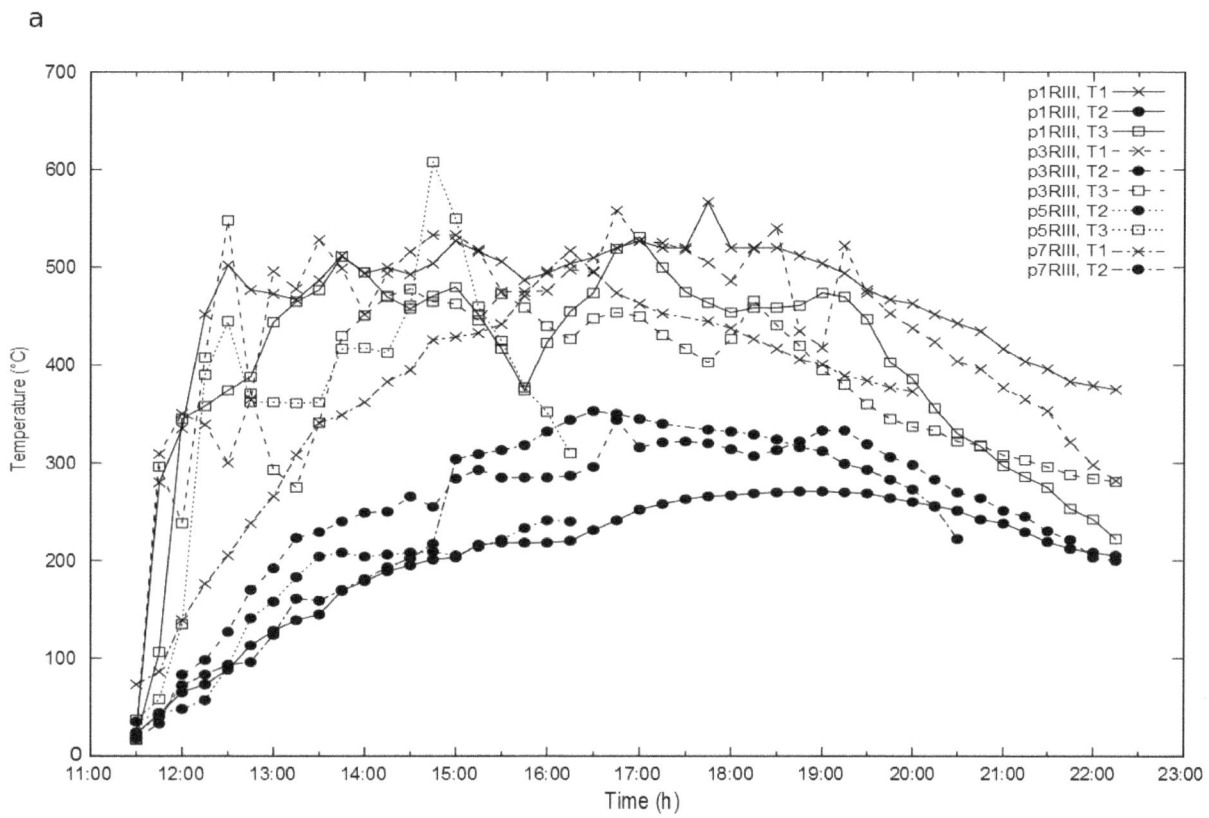

b

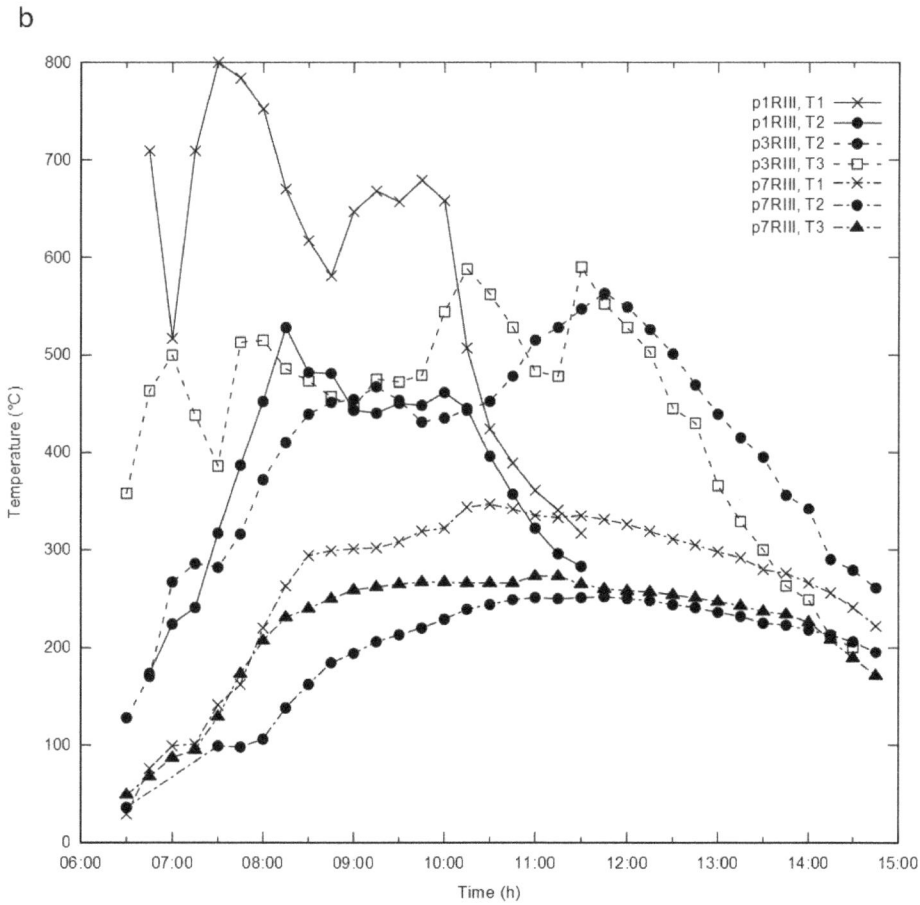

Fig. 5.8 A combined diagram of temperature distribution of forms p1RIII, p3RIII, p5RIII and p7RIII during a) the first firing episode; b) the second firing episode.

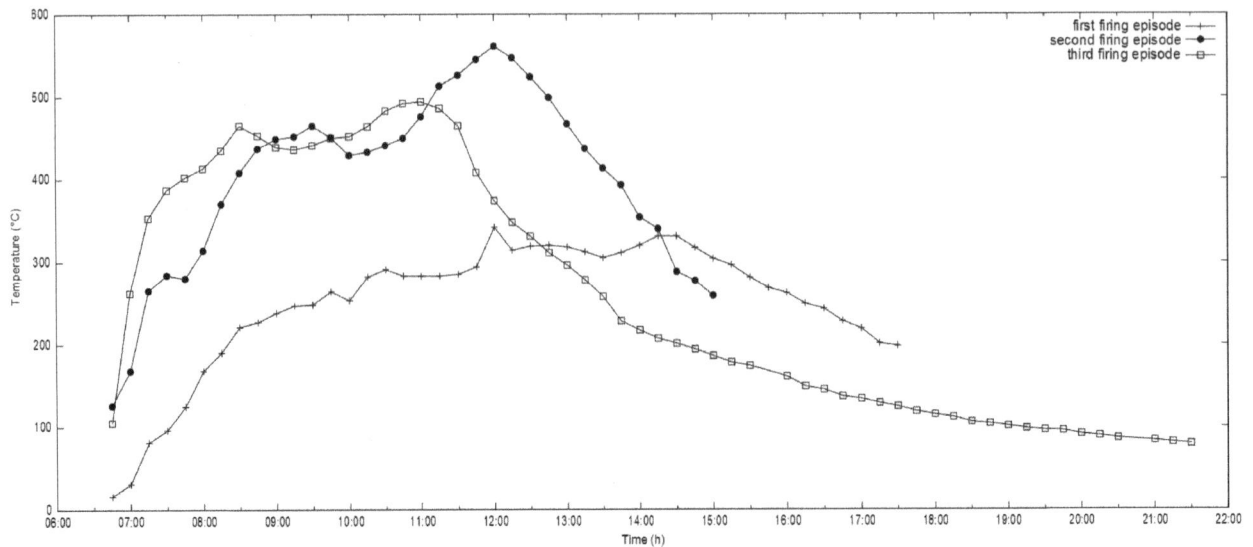

Fig. 5.9 A combined diagram of temperature distribution in T2 point of p3RIII during the first, the second and the third firing episode.

at top, black in between and brown at bottom) and looked exactly the same as the section through the clay of the preceding hollow (j2RIII).

The results

1. Temperature. The temperature of the fire during the firing process is not stable and largely dependent on atmospheric factors. The mean temperature of the fire is 641.37°C. The mean temperature at point T0 during firing made using embers only without the participation of fire does not exceed 500°C. Use of animal bone for fuel results in the decrease of the mean firing temperature to 500°C.

During firing substantial differences are noted within the clay form depending on the point at which they are measured. The clay of the clay hearth is heated in a non-uniform manner, subjected as it is to the action of high temperature only from the top. This fact combined with the low thermal conduction of clay causes the temperature of layers found lower down to be lower by 100°C–200°C than in the layer of clay directly in contact with the fire. During firing the clay at the bottom of the clay hearth is subject to steady heating and it is conceivable that if the firing lasted sufficiently long (perhaps for even more than 24 hours) temperatures of the clay in the entire form would have become uniform.

At the same time, it is worth noting that even the layer of clay immediately in contact with the fire never achieves a temperature equal to the temperature of the fire itself. The clay at top T1, next to the fire, heats rapidly but remains on average lower by 225°C than the temperature T0 (fig.5.8). The difference of mean temperatures T1 during firing I and II is 84°C.

Temperature T3 is to a large extent susceptible to changes in the temperature of the fire (T0). The mean value of T3 is ca. 300°C. The most stable temperature prevails at the bottom of the clay form, at point T2. It is also the least affected by changes in the temperature of the fire. Temperature T2 during first firing is relatively low, on average at ca. 180°C and does not exceed 250°C (fig.5.8). Temperature increase is insubstantial and lasts until the end of firing, or even longer, suggesting that the temperature of the clay could continue to grow in conditions of a longer firing.

Consequently, whereas the temperature of the fire is in the range of 700–900°C, the temperature of the upper layers of the clay hearth ranges between 550 and 650°C, while the temperature of the bottom layers, in direct contact with the ground–between 300 and 400°C (fig.5.8).

A form fired in wet conditions heats at a slower rate, during a firing process of several hours' duration it achieves a maximum temperature of around 300°C. Clay fired after drying using open fire becomes heated most quickly. In such a case over a period of two hours the clay achieves a temperature of around 300°C. During a firing of several hours' duration the clay is heated to around 400°C–500°C. In the course of experiments the author was unable to heat the clay under the surface of the hearth to a temperature higher than 680°C.

In the course of a series of firing episodes the clay heats in the same manner, irrespective of whether the form was fired for the first time as wet or dry. Throughout each successive firing the clay took a shorter time to achieve the maximum temperature. During the second firing the temperature in the clay achieved during the first two hours of firing was equal to the maximum temperature achieved during firing I (fig.5.9). From this point on the temperature continues to increase but does not exceed 600°C. After reaching around 500°C the diagram stabilises and there is no further increase. The mean temperature during the second firing is ca. 320°C.

2. The experiment results in detail. Burying the fire with earth (p1RIII–firing II, p3RIII–firing III) caused:

- oxidation of the outer layer of clay to a red hue;
- development of a layer of reduced clay grey in hue on the inside of the form;
- sustaining the embers for a dozen odd hours after burying the fire;
- transformation of the wood fuel burnt during the firing to charcoal in conditions of cut off oxygen supply.

In clay hearths modelled over a form which had been fired earlier (p4RIII):

- The clay on the outer side had a better supply of oxygen which makes it possible to fire in an oxidising atmosphere.

- The form found underneath is not subjected to excessively high temperatures (during firing with embers this was around 200°C).

The firing of a wet form made of clay originating from Klissoura has no effect on the temperatures in the clay. The clay heats at the same rate as clay fired after drying (results of a single experiment).

When fired wet, in clay forms made of clays other than the clay from Klissoura, the clay was slower to take on the heat from the fire, and stayed wet even after the firing episode was over.

The cross–section made through the clay found underneath the fire, when the fire is made directly over a clayey substrate, does not correspond in its appearance to sections made through forms discovered at Klissoura. The clay in the profile consists of three layers: red on the top, black in between, and grey–brown in the layer of unfired clay at bottom.

CHAPTER 6

FOURTH SERIES OF EXPERIMENTS

The fourth series of experiments was carried out in February 2008 in a rock shelter found about 20 metres NE and 10 metres above Klissoura Cave 1. This had been the location of the second series of experiments made in 2006.

During the IV series of experiments 15 clay forms were built, used in a total of 45 firing episodes. All the experiments had been planned beforehand so that with each successive experiment there would be a change of not more than one variable. The general assumptions foresaw the making of experiments in five cycles, each of which was to assist in answering a specific question.

1. The first cycle involved the making and firing of:
- one wet form (p2KIV) and two dried forms (p6KIV and p7KIV), using an open fire made on top of the form;
- one wet form (p1KIV, p4KIV) and one dried form (p5KIV), using embers (fig.6.1).

The firing of each of the named forms was to be repeated three or four times. Form (p7KIV) was to be fired without being lifted after each firing to document both its sides. This was to test whether the removal each time of the form each time from the ground after firing to document the appearance of its underside increased the inflow of oxygen and to what extent it affects the better oxidation of the surface of the clay.

2. The second cycle made it necessary to build two forms for firing, without being allowed to dry (p3KIV) and after drying (p10KIV), several times, using a very hot fire for a short time, after which the form would be swept clean of the embers and ashes and left to cool to imitate a situation in which a form might be used as a place for roasting or boiling (fig.6.2).

3. The assumption adopted for the third cycle was to have two forms built outside a hollow made in the ground (p11KIV, p12KIV) and fire them directly using an open fire.

4. In the fourth cycle two forms were to be fired, without being allowed to dry (p8KIV) and when dried (p9KIV), using an open fire and as a next step, buried under a layer of earth to assess the degree of oxidation or reduction of the clay (fig.6.3). Previously, experiments in which the fire had been buried under a layer of earth had been made using forms built of local clays, during their second or third firing (series III of experiments made in Romania) which could have affected the colour of the clay. Therefore it seemed justified to make a similar

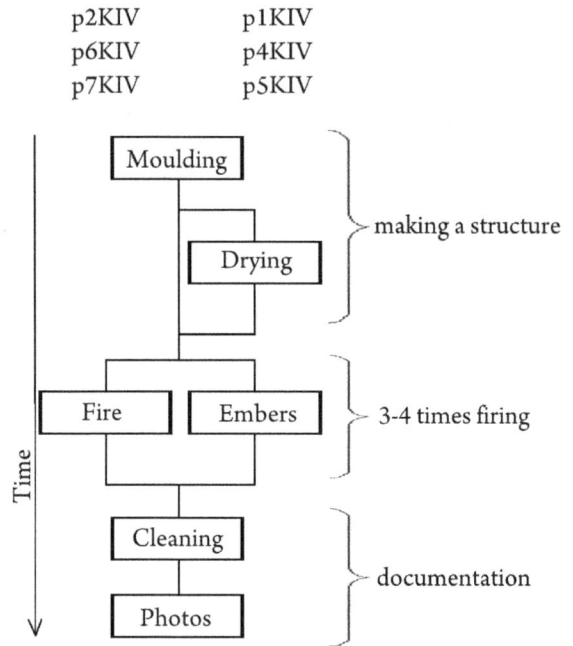

Fig. 6.1 Scheme of the first cycle of experiments including p1KIV, p2IV, p4KIV, p5KIV, p6KIV and p7KIV.

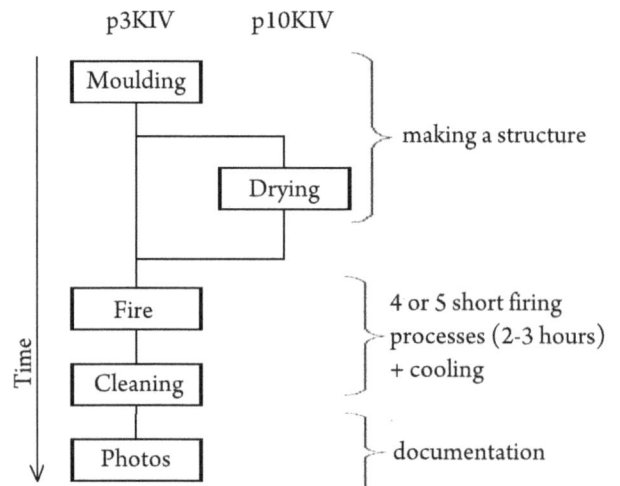

Fig. 6.2 Scheme of the second cycle of experiments including p3KIV and p10KIV.

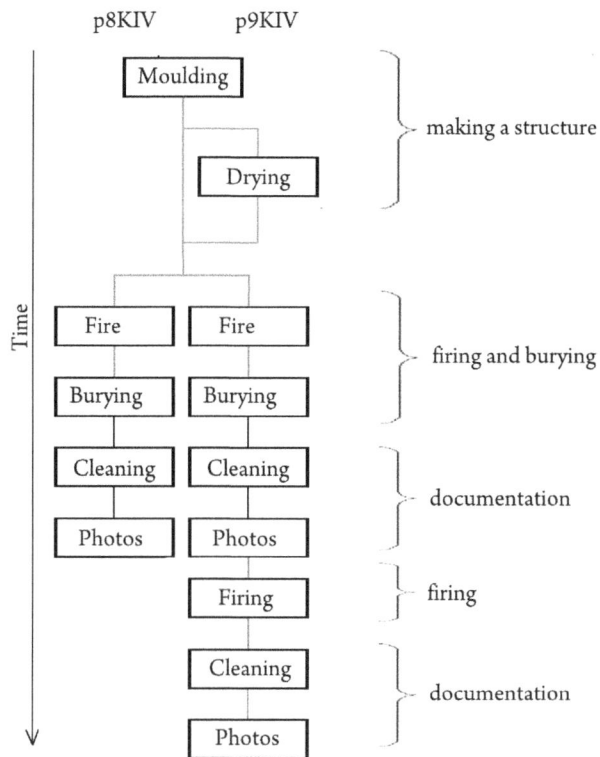

p8KIV   p9KIV

- Moulding } making a structure
- Drying

- Fire / Fire } firing and burying
- Burying / Burying

- Cleaning / Cleaning } documentation
- Photos / Photos

- Firing } firing

- Cleaning } documentation
- Photos

Fig. 6.3 Scheme of the fourth cycle of experiments including P8KIV and p9KIV.

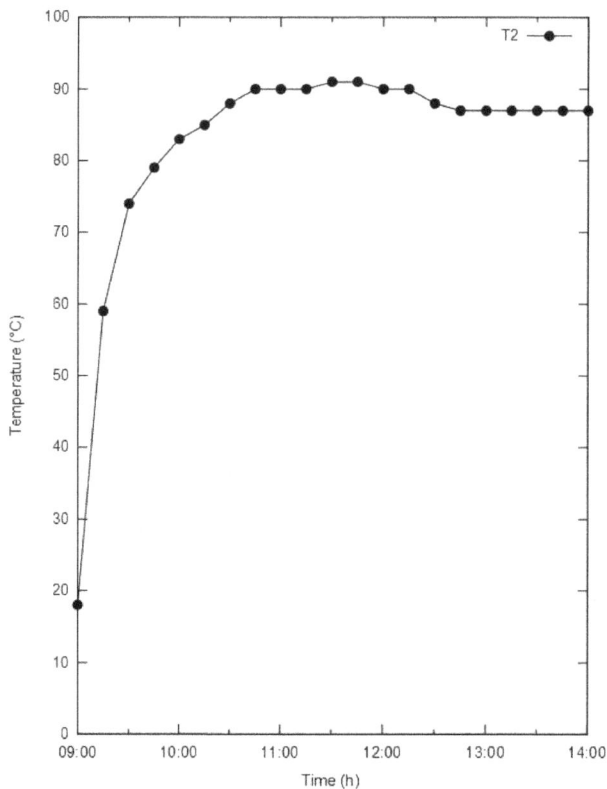

Fig. 6.4 Temperature distribution in form p1KIV during the first firing episode (T2 temperature on the bottom of the clay structure).

experiment with unfired forms and ones built of *terra rosa* clay.

5. The fifth cycle aimed on testing alternative methods of building the clay forms, testing their usefulness and ergonomics. The method of building the clay structures (p13KIV and p14KIV) is described in detail under the relevant heading below.

While the experiments were in progress it seemed justified to build still another form (p15KIV) which was fired once without being allowed to dry using an open fire (to observe colour change of the clay on the underside after a single firing).

All the forms were built of clay taken from a slope rising over the river bed some 1.5km E of the cave. According to the definition adopted in 2006 this was no. 2 clay.

During firing because of shortage of thermocouples it was decided to discontinue measuring the temperature of the fire itself.

P1KIV

This form had a diameter of 35x37cm, was nearly flat, its walls protruded over the surface of the bottom by only ca. 1cm. Its thickness was about 2cm. When the form was ready a temperature sensor was installed at point T2 (within the clay) after which the form was spread over with hot embers. They were replenished successively during firing. Temperature readouts were made over 6 hours. For the first two and a half hours the temperature of the clay continued to rise until it reached a maximum value of 91.4°C (fig.6.4). From this time on, temperature started to drop off gradually and very slowly, on average by 0.38°C (σ=0.61) every 15 minutes. After six hours of firing the temperature of the clay was 87.6°C.

During firing the thermocouple became dislodged from the place in which it had been installed and had to be reinserted. Because the firing was still in progress and the form was buried under a layer of embers it was very difficult to reinstall the sensor in exactly its original place. The tip of the thermocouple was inserted under the clay in a place as close as possible to the point of the earlier readouts. The difference in the next readout after this was 0.7°C which suggested that readouts which followed are correct and may be tied into a single sequence.

During the firing the form became fissured on its upper surface and developed a layer of ash there, something which would be observed in all the experiments. The colour of the clay in the entire cross–section (also from below) had not been altered by the heat of the firing and continued to be reddish–brown. Organic particles in the fired clay had not burnt away because the temperature of the clay had not been higher than 100°C. After a fragment of the form p1KIV was placed in water the clay reverted fully to its original state and could be used to make a new form.

29

Because the form had become fissured it was decided to discontinue further firing episodes.

P2KIV

This form was built over a clay structure surviving from the II series of experiments (2006). This earlier clay form was larger so the form p2KIV rested entirely within this structure. Its diameter was 32cm, thickness of ca. 2cm. The finished form was almost flat. A tunnel was made in the clay of the form to insert a thermocouple for the duration of the firing. At first the temperature was measured within the clay, closer to the bottom, by introducing the thermocouple into the tunnel. However, during the third firing episode the tunnel became fractured and the form at this point crumbled. During the third and fourth firing the thermocouple was inserted underneath the clay.

First firing

The finished form was fired without being allowed to dry using an open fire made on top of it. During the first firing measurements were made of the temperature of the fire and temperature at point T1/T2.

The fire burnt for seven hours. After this time no further temperature readouts were made and the fire was left to burn itself out over the form. During the firing temperature was subject to cyclical fluctuation associated with firing and adding wood to the fire (fig.6.5a). The temperature of the fire did not pass the 750°C mark and the average value was 619.1°C. The temperature of the clay continued to increase for the entire duration of the firing. For the first three hours the curve of increase was consistent with curves obtained for firing episodes made with wet forms: for the first half hour there was a rapid increase in temperature to around 90°C, followed, over the next two and a half hours, be a very slow temperature increase to around 110°C. During this time water within the clay evaporated. After passing the mark of ca. 110°C the temperature started to rise consistently with the curve obtained when firing dried forms, on average by 7.07°C (σ=1.11) every 15 minutes (fig.6.5a).

The clay reached the maximum temperature of 238.3°C seven hours into the firing episode. The fire had stopped burning about half an hour before the taking of the last readouts.

The next morning–12.5 hours after end of the firing, the embers continued to smoulder over the form. The temperature of the clay was measured at two points on its surface–T0/T1, and the point of taking earlier readouts–T1/T2. On the surface the clay had a temperature of 134.8°C, whereas at point T1/T2–it was 303.1°C. This last readout may be incorrect because no similarly high temperature was obtained during earlier experiments 12 hours after the ending of the firing. If, however, this result is correct it would mean, consistently with the curves of previous firing episodes, that the clay had

reached a maximum temperature of ca. 380–400°C six hours after the end of this firing episode.

After the last readout was taken the form was swept clean of the remaining embers and ashes. After this the temperature of the clay started to drop rapidly. At the time of starting the next firing (about half an hour later) the temperature of the clay was 240.3°C.

After the first firing the top of the clay had turned black in colour, only next to the rim some fragments had turned red (Pl.2.3). It was decided to forego lifting the form from the ground to examine the colour of its underside because this threatened to cause disintegration of the form which had become quite fissured. Observation of the colour on the underside of the form was possible only near the rims where the clay had touched the clay hearth from the 2006 experiments. In these places the clay had turned black in colour.

Second firing

During the second firing readouts were taken only at point T1/T2. The firing lasted five and a half hours. After this time the fire was left to go out and temperature was measured over the next half an hour. The temperature of the clay after the fire had been made started to increase rapidly and after 30 minutes reached the value of 398.6°C, and an hour into the firing episode–484.8°C. This rapid temperature increase definitely had been caused on the one hand by the initial temperature 240.3°C of the form at the outset of the firing (fig.6.5b), on the other, by the considerably fissured condition of the clay which made it possible for the heat to penetrate deeper into the clay form. After reaching the value of 484.8°C the temperature of the clay started to gradually drop off even though the size of the fire was maintained the same and wood continued to be added. It seems that the temperature decrease may have been caused by accumulation of ashes on the surface of the form. The layer of ashes and embers, as a rule with a temperature of around 450°C, cut the clay off from the heat of the fire which on average has a temperature higher by 200–300°C. A very similar process was observed later with other firing episodes using other forms, when the form continued to heat substantially until it accumulated a layer of embers on top, after which time the temperature started to drop off or remained stable, on a slightly lower level. This situation was observed only in relation to successive firing episodes, but not the first firing, when the clay only starts to heat and slowly reaches a temperature of over 300°C.

After the maximum temperature of the clay was reached it remained on a similar level of 470–430°C, nevertheless, with an observable downward tendency (fig.6.5b). Average temperature decrease was 2.91°C (σ=7.71) every 15 minutes, but until the end of the firing the temperature did not drop below the 400°C mark.

After the firing was over the fire was left to go out. The next morning, after 18 hours from the end of the firing, only hot ashes remained on top of the form, with no

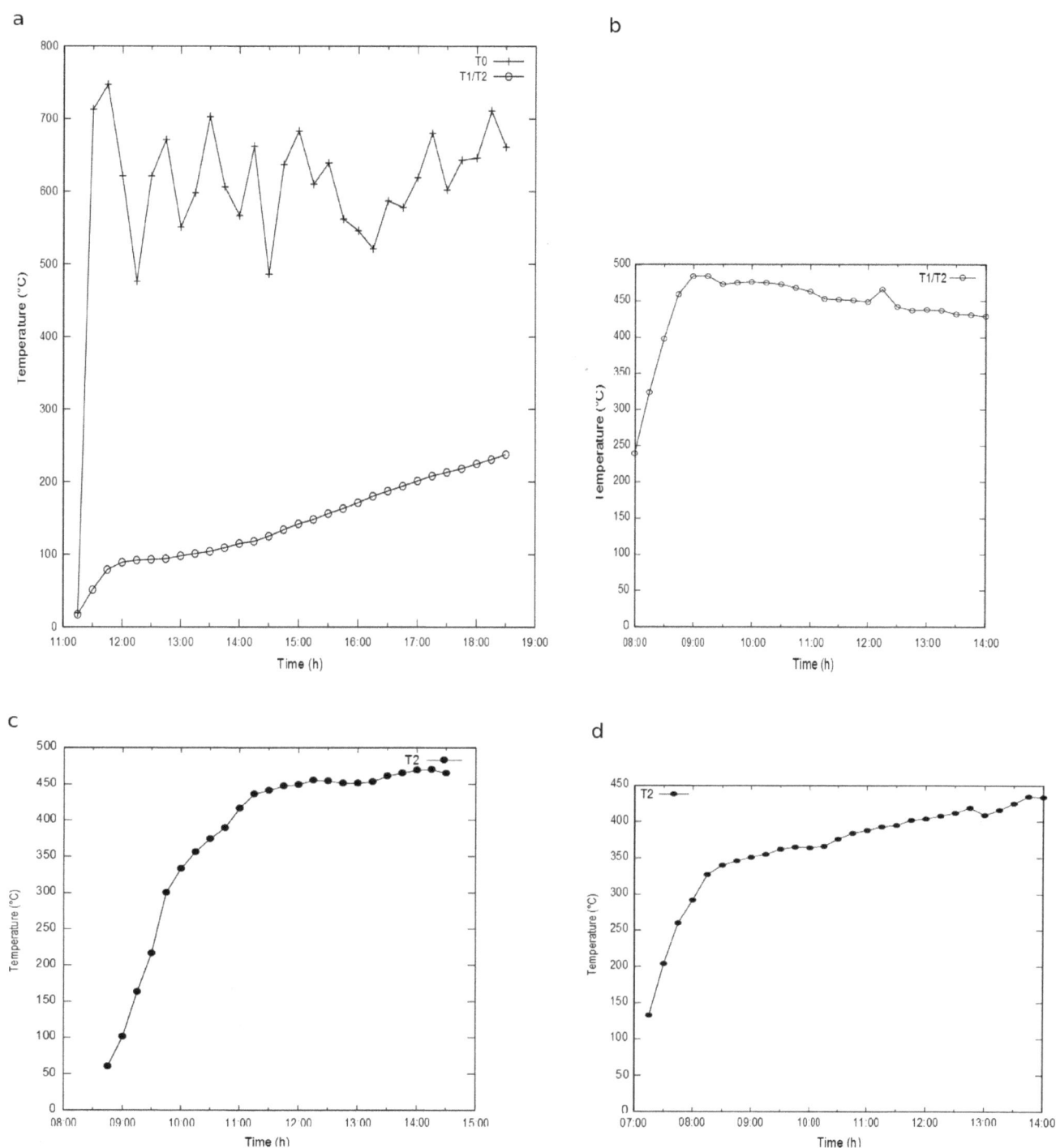

Fig. 6.5 Temperature distribution in form p2KIV during a) the first firing episode, b) the second firing episode, c) the third firing episode d) the fourth firing episode (T0–temperature of the fire; T1/T2–temperature of the clay midway in the cross–section of the clay hearth; T2–temperature on the bottom of the clay structure).

embers. The temperature of the surface of the clay (T1) was at this time 76.1°C, whereas the temperature at the point of earlier readouts (T1/T2) was 87.6°C. After the form had been swept clean of the ashes its appearance was recorded. The clay over almost the entire upper surface had turned red except for a small fragment at the very centre of the form (Pl.2.3).As in case of the first firing, a decision was taken not to lift the form from the ground. However, at the point where the tunnel for the thermocouple had fractured and crumbled away, it was

possible to examine the appearance of the clay form in cross–section. At this point the clay on its underside had turned red in colour.

Third firing

The third firing started the same day, before the clay had had time to cool completely. At the time when a new fire was made the clay had a temperature of 60°C. Because the tunnel for inserting the thermocouple had fractured it was decided to change the point of readout installing it slightly deeper inside the form (T2). The firing lasted five hours. After this time, as with the preceding firing episodes, the fire was left to go out. In case of this firing it was decided to successively remove the embers which were forming over the form and transfer them to p4KIV, which was at this time being fired using embers. The aim of this procedure was to see what would be the temperature curve in a situation where no ashes or embers are allowed to accumulate on the surface of the clay hearth.

During the entire firing episode the temperature of the clay rose steadily until it reached the maximum value of 470.4°C at the time when the firing came to an end (fig.6.5c). Temperature increase occurred in three stages. To reach the value of 300°C the temperature increased on average by 60.18°C (σ=17.92) every 15 minutes. After reaching this value the rate of increase became slower and for the next one and a half hours it was at 22.65°C (σ=6.39) every 15 minutes, until reaching the value of 436.6°C. From this time on until the end of the firing the rate of temperature increase rose on average by 2.82°C (σ=3.11) every 15 minutes and was characterised by some negligible fluctuation.

After about 15 minutes after the flames had disappeared the temperature of the clay started slowly to drop off. The next morning the temperature of the clay was measured but a more accurate insertion of the sensor was not possible because the form was buried at this time under a layer of ashes (sweeping it clean of the ashes would have caused a very rapid reduction of temperature). The readout at point T1/T2 was 98°C.

After sweeping out the ashes the whole clay form was recorded which, as it seemed from observation of the rim and eroded places, had turned red over its entire surface, both on its upper face and on the underside.

Fourth firing

The fourth firing was made the last day of the experiments so in order to let the form cool and be recorded it had to be swept clean of the embers. The sensor was installed at point T2 within the clay, the firing episode lasted seven hours. Since this firing episode was carried out two days after the previous one, at the time when the fire was being made the temperature of the clay was the same as its surroundings (around 10°C).

The temperature diagram (fig.6.5d) shows that the increase in temperature was in two stages. Over the first hour the rate of increase was very high and measured every 15 minutes was respectively, 70°C, 55°C, 32°C, 34°C, 13°C, until it reached 340.8°C. From this time on, the rate of increase levelled off considerably and over the next 4 hours was 4.62°C (σ=2.67) for every 15 minutes. The maximum value of 435.0°C was achieved after six and a half hours, right before the fire was swept out.

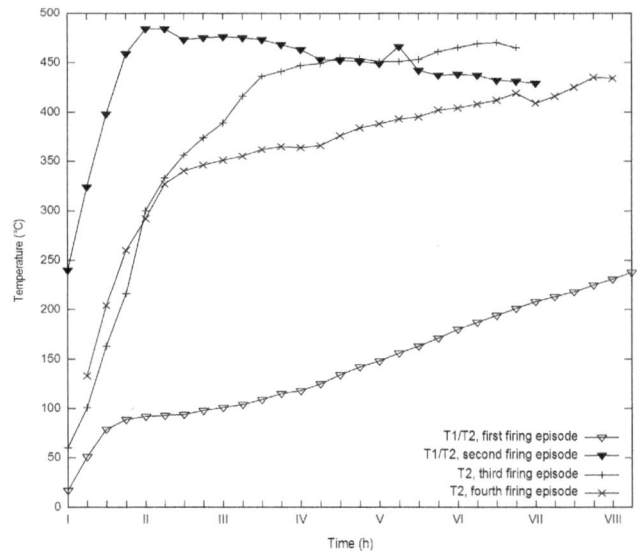

Fig. 6.6 A combined diagram of temperature distribution in form p2KIV during all the firing episodes (T1/T2–temperature of the clay midway in the cross–section of the clay heart; T2–temperature on the bottom of the clay structure).

After the fourth firing the clay remained red in colour over its entire surface (Pl.2.2,3). After the form cooled it was possible to attempt to lift it out from the 2006 clay hearth to document the appearance also of its underside. Unfortunately, the seriously fissured condition of the clay caused the form to disintegrate during lifting. On its underside the entire surface of the clay form had turned red. The 2006 form overlain by p2KIV had a red upper surface but at bottom had partly turned black and partly red.

Conclusion

A composite diagram of all the firing episodes (fig.6.6) shows that with each new firing there was an increase not only in the maximum temperature achieved but also in the rate of temperature increase starting from the beginning of the firing. A departure from this pattern was shown by the second firing which had started when the form was still very hot–240°C. The making of a fire caused a very rapid increase in temperature of the clay to almost 500°C. After reaching this level the temperature started to slowly drop off.

P3KIV

The aim of making this form, similarly as with p10KIV, was to see whether a repeated short and intensive firing used to heat the form, followed every time by sweeping the form clean of the embers and letting it cool off, would affect the colour of the clay after firing. This firing method was meant to imitate a situation in which the forms would have been used as a place for roasting foodstuffs over the heated surface of the clay.

The diameter of the form p3KIV was 32x28cm, its thickness–2–2.5cm. The form was placed within a small hollow so that the difference between the level of the rim and the bottom of the form was 3cm.

The form was fired immediately after being built without being allowed to dry. Then came four other brief firing episodes, each lasting 2–3 hours. During the firing the temperature of the clay or the temperature of the fire were not regulated, although an attempt was made for the fire to be as hot as possible so that it would heat the form to a maximum. After each firing the fire was raked out, the form swept clean of the embers and ashes, leaving its surface clear in order to let it cool.

During the first firing, which lasted three hours, there was a small rain which speeded up the process of cooling of the form. The two succeeding firing episodes lasted two hours each. Between the second and the third firing there was a two hours' break to allow the form to cool.

After the second firing the entire upper surface of the form had turned black except for small areas near the rim. The entire form was very heavily fissured which definitely was the result of firing the clay when still wet. A part of the upper surface started to spall, exposing a dark brown layer of clay underneath. After the third firing the area on the upper surface black in colour contracted to the centre of the form and the area next to the rim had turned red. On its underside, the form had turned black whereas on the surface near the rim it became red.

The next day the fourth and the fifth firing were carried out. In between the form was swept clean of the embers and left to cool. Lifted from the ground after the fifth firing the form broke into several fragments. On its underside it was completely black. Viewed in cross–section this layer was found to have a thickness of ca. 3–4mm. In cross–section the clay had turned dark brown. The red oxidised surface formed a slender layer at top of the upper face of the form next to the rim. This appearance of the clay after firing could have been caused by a relatively great depth of the form as compared to its diameter which caused the fire to cover the form entirely during the firing and the accumulating embers and ashes to cover nearly the entire surface of the form.

P4KIV

The diameter of the form was 37x39cm, its thickness at bottom and next to the rim respectively, 4cm and 3cm. Its depth was 7cm. Immediately after it was built the first firing episode was started. The form was subjected to a total of four firing episodes, during each of them it was spread over with embers which were replenished during firing. When using this method of firing (with embers) it is difficult to determine the limits and duration of the firing. For this reason the only information given here is about the time during which the embers were replenished and the time when this was discontinued and the embers were left to go out. After the firing ended the form and the embers were each time left until the next morning, when the ashes and, possibly, also the embers were raked and swept out from the form.

The first firing episode started when the form was still wet. The clay was spread over with embers which were replenished an hour after starting the firing. The next morning, 18 hours after the last time when the embers were replenished, the temperature at point T2 was 85.1°C and the embers continued to smoulder within the form. After the form had been swept clean and left to cool a little, the second firing was started. Previous to this the appearance of the upper face of the clay form was recorded. In view of its considerably fissured condition the form was not lifted from the ground to examine the appearance of its underside. The clay of the entire upper surface had turned beige in colour, with no traces of black.

Over the first 30 minutes of the second firing readouts of the temperature of the clay were made at point T2. The temperature continued to rise, reaching after half an hour the value of 124.1°C. After this time further readouts were discontinued. Embers were replenished during two hours after the start of the firing.

The next morning, 22 hours after the last replenishing of the embers, the form was still warm and filled with ashes, the embers had fully gone out. After the inside of the form was swept clean of the ashes the appearance of its upper surface was recorded. The colour of the clay was hard to examine due to the presence of a slender layer of ashes which had penetrated inside the fissures and the uneven surface of the clay. In places where the clay had flaked off, dark brown colour of the interior of the clay mass was visible.

During the third firing episode the embers were replenished several times over 5 hours. After this time the firing the temperature of the clay was measured. Temperature T0/T1 measured on the surface of the form was at this time 285.0°C, and the temperature at point T2–185.5°C. After taking this readout the embers were not replenished any longer and left to go out. The next morning, 18 hours after the last readout, the embers continued to smoulder inside the form whereas the temperature of the clay had reached to the following values: T0/T1–348.3°C, T2–219.4°C. May it be noted that the readout T0/T1 was made by touching the tip of the sensor to the surface of the clay and may have been brought up by the temperature of the embers. Therefore, the readouts taken at point T2 found on the bottom surface of the clay may be more reliable.

After the third firing the clay on the surface in some places, mainly at centre of the form, had turned black. Most of the surface continued to be coated with a slender layer of ashes, which made it difficult to examine the colour of the clay itself. In places where the clay had spalled it continued to be dark brown, similarly as after the first and the second firing.

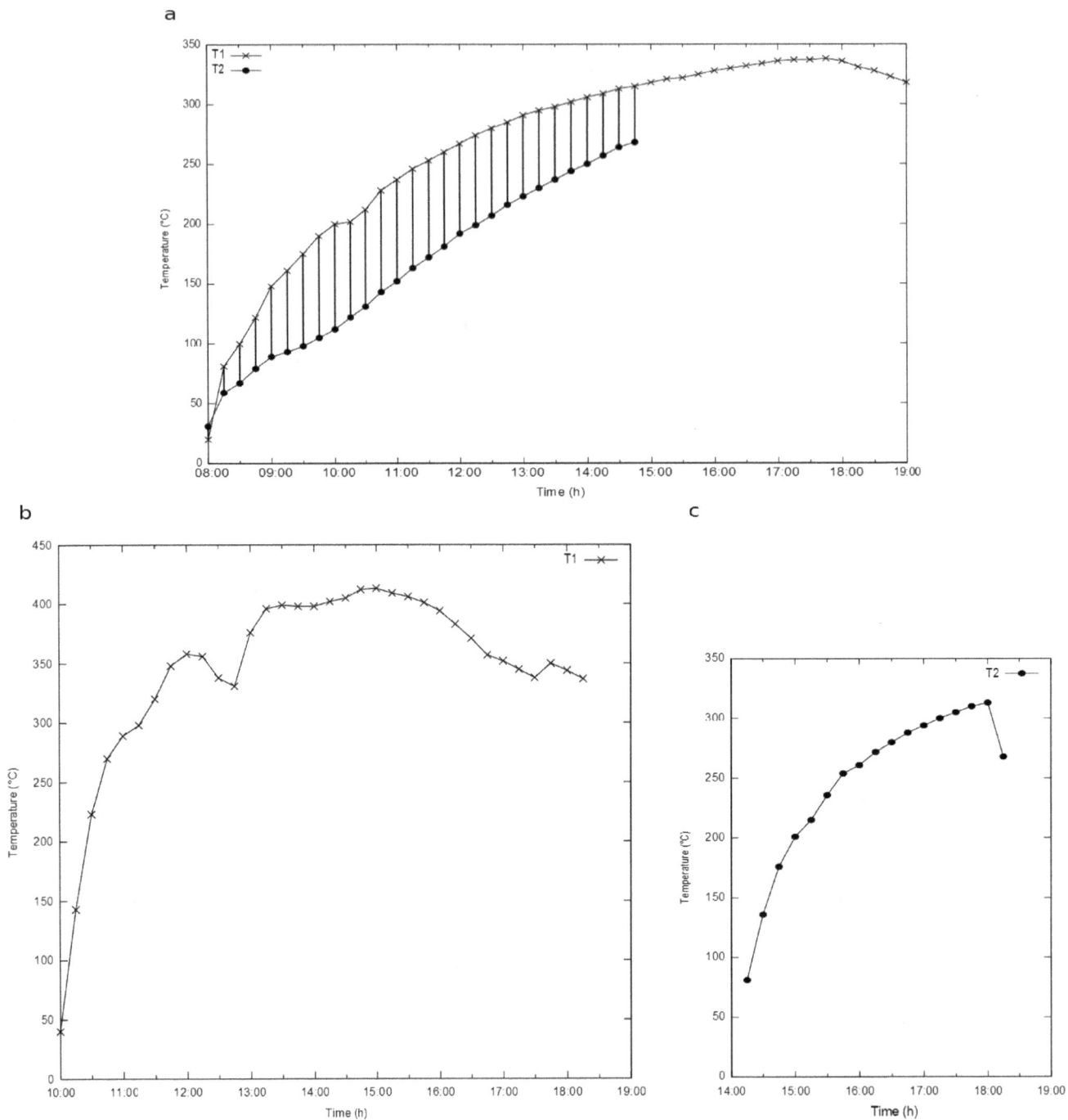

Fig. 6.7 Temperature distribution in form p5KIV during a) the first firing episode, b) the second firing episode, c) the third firing episode (T1–temperature just under the surface–not more than 5mm; T2–temperature on the bottom of the clay structure).

The last, fourth firing episode lasted about 5 hours. After this time the temperature of the clay was measured at point T2 and a value of 280.5°C obtained.

The next day the form was swept clean of the ashes and embers and its appearance recorded, both from the top and from the bottom as well as in cross–section.

The clay on the upper surface remained black at centre. Next to the rims it had turned red–dark brown, whereas on the underside at the centre of the form it was red–dark brown. Black colour, not too intensive in any case, appeared only next to the rims. In cross–section the form was almost entirely red–brown, except for a slender 2–3mm layer found at the very top of the upper face of the form (Pl.2.1). In some places in the cross–section were visible dark spots left by burnt out organic matter. A fragment of the clay placed in water reverted almost fully to its original state except for a slender layer found on the upper surface of the form.

P5KIV

This form and experiments it was part of belonged to the first cycle. According to plan, form P5KIV was allowed to dry and was fired using embers. The diameter of the form was 30x32cm, thickness of its bottom–2–3cm. The structure had a depth of 4cm. After being built it was left to dry for three days.

First firing

The form was spread with embers which were replenished in stages over the next two hours. During the firing the temperature of the clay was measured at two points–T1 and T2. After almost seven hours into this firing episode the temperature sensor inserted at point T2 was taken out, leaving only the readout T1.

The temperature of the clay continued to rise over the next three hours, reaching after nearly ten hours of this firing episode (eight hours from the last replenishing of the embers), a value of 338.5°C. The rate of temperature increase over the first two and a half hours had been dependent, to a considerable extent, on the replenishing of the embers. Successive readouts and the curve of temperature increase (fig.6.7a) shows that 15–30 minutes after the addition of new embers the temperature started to rise with a greater speed. This increase lasted for around half an hour, after which the rate of increase dropped off until the next addition of embers. The delay in the heat reaction of the clay was, as can be seen from the diagram, one of about 15–30 minutes.

After the embers were replenished for the last time the temperature continued to rise, on average by 3.95°C (σ=2.47) every 15 minutes, but the rate of increase gradually dropped off–on average by 0.34°C (σ=0.87) every 15 minutes (fig.6.7a). After ten hours of firing the temperature started to decrease quite uniformly, by 4.08°C (σ=1.40) every 15 minutes. After the last readouts were made the form was left for the night to cool.

The next day temperature was measured 23.5 hours from the last replenishing of the embers. The temperature at point T1 was 111.7°C, at point T2–68.9°C. The embers had fully gone out during the night and only the ashes remained on top of the form.

After the form was swept clean of the ashes the appearance of both its sides could be recorded. The form could be lifted from the ground because the clay had not fissured. On the upper face of the form, despite careful sweeping, there was still a slender layer of ashes. The clay at top was a non–uniform colour. Next to the rims it was more red, at centre, black. On its underside, the form was entirely black. Only next to the rim, on one side, the colour of the clay had turned dark brown (This was on the same side where at top the form had turned red).

Second firing

After the previous firing the form had been left to cool over the night. The next morning it was swept clean of the embers which had not gone out during the night. During the firing the temperature of the clay was measured at point T1.

After the second firing the upper surface of the clay had oxidised to a greater extent, only the centre of the form remained black. From the bottom the clay remained almost entirely black, with small dark brown at centre and by the rim. In cross–section which was exposed by the crumbling away of a small fragment of the rim, the form was non–uniform black–dark brown. Additionally, on the upper surface there was a slender 1–8mm layer of black colour.

Third firing

This firing lasted for four hours. During the firing the temperature was measured at point T2 because the tunnel made for inserting the sensor at point T1 had fractured. When the first portion of burning embers was added the clay had fully cooled off. The embers were added in stages over the first two hours of firing; for the next two hours only observation of the changes in temperature were made.

Initially, the temperature of the clay increased quite rapidly. The rate of increase grew after each addition of new embers (fig.6.7c). The first two hours into the firing the average increase of temperature in the clay was 20.76°C (σ=15.89) for every 15 minutes, but the rate of increase gradually levelled off. After the last addition of the embers, the temperature of the clay continued to rise, but on average only by 5.02°C (σ=1.03) every 15 minutes.

Four hours into the firing episode all the embers remaining over the form were swept out and the form was left to cool. After the third firing the clay on the upper surface remained black at centre and red next to the rims. The underside of the form was entirely black. After breaking the clay its cross–section was exposed, dark brown in colour, except for a very slender, about 1–2 mm layer of black on the bottom side of the form. A fragment of the clay was placed in water but it did not dissolve and only started to disintegrate to a negligible extent as a result of saturation.

Conclusion

Because of the limited number of sensors we only have the following readouts: from T1, from firing I and II, and from T2, from firing I and III. A comparison of temperature diagrams from successive firing episodes suggests that with each successive firing the temperature of the clay increased at both points, T1 and T2 (fig.6.8). There was also an increase in the rate of heating the clay after starting the firing.

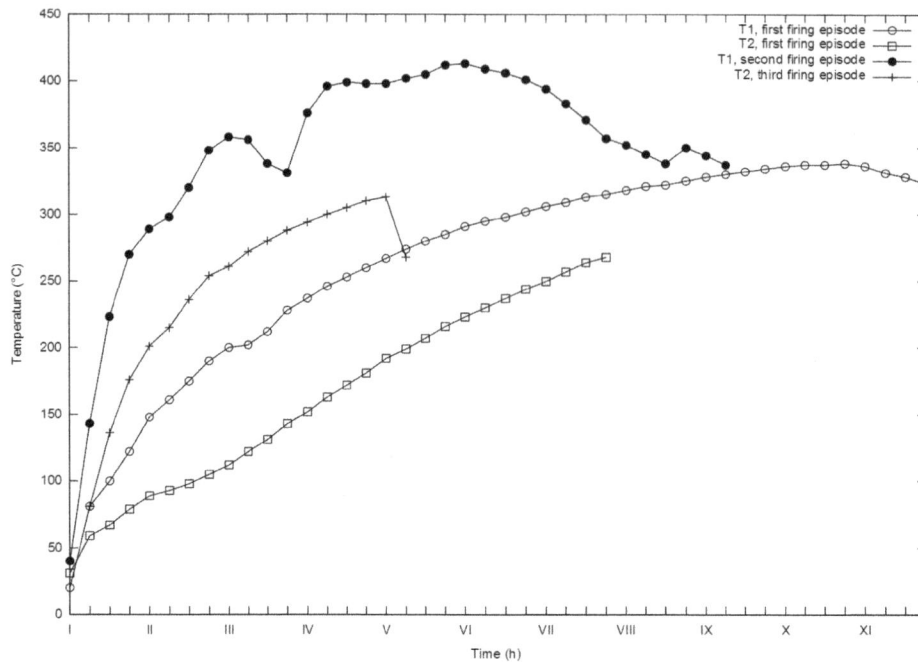

Fig. 6.8 A combined diagram of temperature distribution in form p5KIV during all the firing episodes (T1–temperature just under the surface–not more than 5mm; T2–temperature on the bottom of the clay structure).

P6KIV

The aim of making this form was to test the appearance of the clay and make temperature readouts over four successive firing episodes during which a dried clay form was exposed to an open fire.

The diameter of the form was 30x32cm, its thickness at bottom and by the rim respectively, 3cm and 2cm. The form was nearly flat, its rim raised over the level of the bottom by a mere 1cm. p6KIV was built on site of an earlier open fire. This place had been cleared but the ground was still warm at the time of making the form which caused the clay to dry much faster but, at the same time, caused its surface to fissure. By the afternoon of the next day the form had become hard and dry so it was decided to carry out the first firing.

First firing

During the first firing temperature readouts were made of the clay at two points: T1 and T2. The first firing took more than five hours. During this time an open fire continued to burn over the form.

Under the surface the temperature of the clay grew over the first 15 minutes by 118.7°C. (fig.6.9a). For the next two hours the rate of increase was on average 27.7°C (σ=18.99) every 15 minutes. When the temperature reached the value of 334.6°C the rate of increase dropped off, on average down to 4.79°C (σ=3.24) every 15 minutes and continued at this level for almost two more hours. After reaching the value of 368.1°C the value of the temperature started to increase more rapidly again, on average by 13.52°C (σ=2.80) every 15 minutes. This

increase may have been caused by the development in the open fire of very good thermic conditions in the form of red hot embers. While the experiments were in progress it was observed that around 5 pm when the wind in the gorge died down the temperature in the fires increased, as expressed by an increase in the temperature of the clay at point T1. For the last hour of the firing the rate of increase dropped off and assumed an average value of 7.13°C (σ=1.84) every 15 minutes. The maximum value of 443.6°C was recorded during the last readout when the fire had started to die down.

The diagram of temperature readouts at point T1 resembles diagrams from other experiments made for forms fired after drying, e.g. p1RIII and p3RIII (Fig. 5.3 and 5.4). In case of temperature diagrams for point T2, the situation looks different. The temperature at bottom of the form increased at a more uniform rate than on the surface of the clay. A feature characteristic for the value of temperature at bottom of the form is a certain delay in thermic reactions to changing conditions. This is well observable early into the firing episode when the temperature started to rise only half an hour after the start of the firing (over the first 15 minutes the increase was a mere 4.5°C). The initial increase was quite substantial–of 34.7°C–but with time the rate of temperature increase dropped off and over the first three hours was on average 10.37°C (σ=2.52) every 15 minutes. After reaching the value of 175.3°C the rate of temperature increase dropped off and for the next two hours was on average 6.92°C (σ=0.70) every 15 minutes. The maximum temperature value of 237.6°C was reached at point T2 during the last readout. The diagram of temperature readouts at point T2 is similar to a great extent to diagrams obtained for clay forms fired when still wet. These are characterised

36

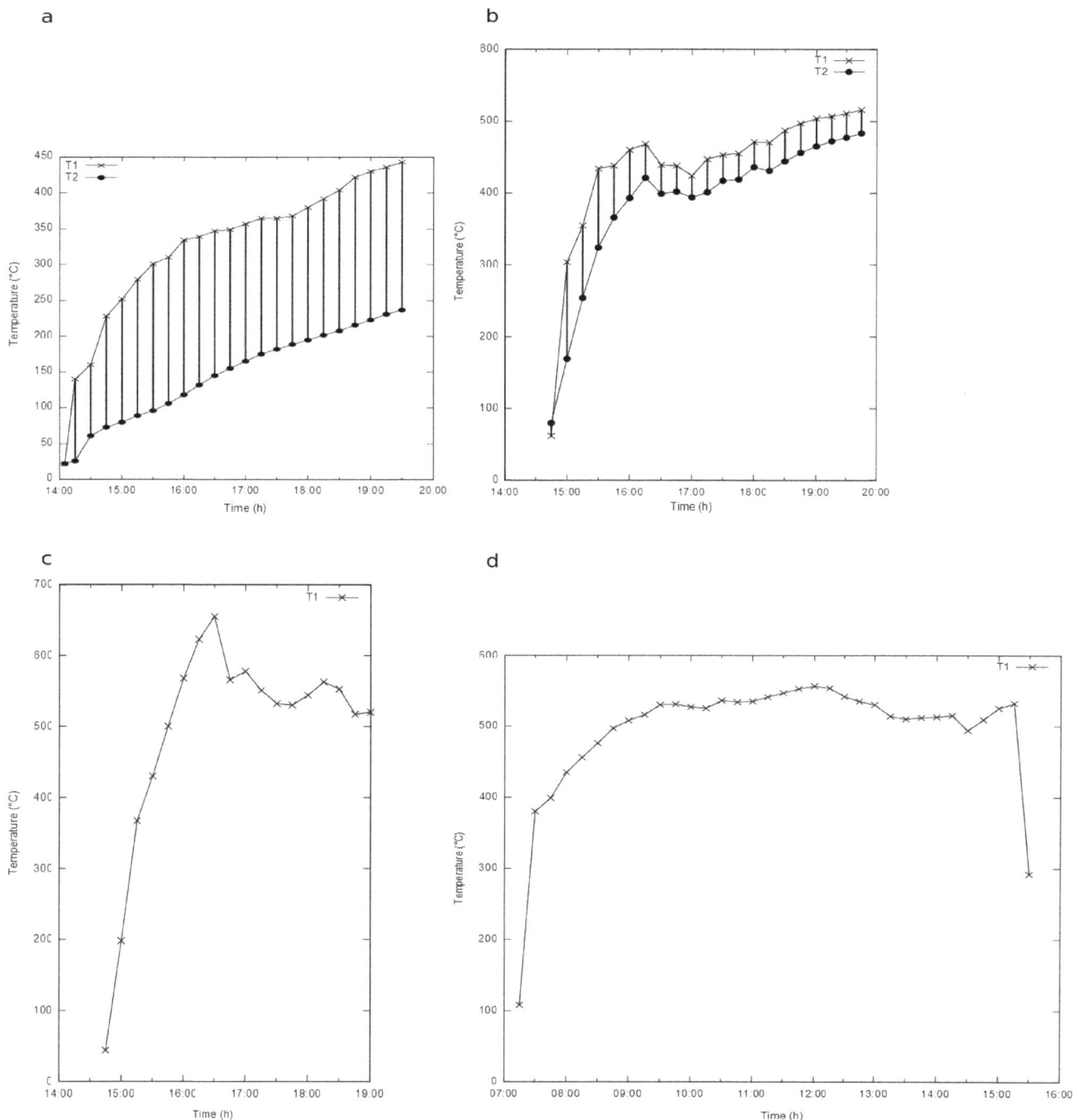

Fig. 6.9 Temperature distribution in form p6KIV during a) the first firing episode, b) the second firing episode, c) the third firing episode d) the fourth firing episode (T1–temperature just under the surface–not more than 5mm; T2–temperature on the bottom of the clay structure).

by a very low increase in temperature and a long period needed for the clay to reach a temperature at which it loses all of its water (over 100°C). Similarity of the temperature curve possibly is tied to the fact that previous to the first firing, the form p6KIV had dried for only 24 hours and may still have been wet on the inside. After the end of the firing the fire was left to burn itself out.

The next day the ashes were swept away and a photographic record of the form was made, both of its top and the underside. At top, the clay had turned red next to

the rim and black at centre, which is quite a typical appearance noted repeatedly in other forms. From the bottom the clay after firing had tuned dark brown.

Second firing

The next day another firing of form p6KIV was started, during which temperature readouts were made. The sensors were placed in the same locations. At the time when the fire was made the clay had not yet had the time to cool off from the first firing, its temperature on the surface was 62°C, at bottom–80°C. From the time when the fire was made the temperature right under the surface of the form had started to grow very rapidly. Over the first 15 minutes it increased 242.5°C. With each temperature readout the rate of increase levelled off but the increase in temperature occurred without a break for the first one and a half hours of the firing, when the clay reached a temperature of 468.5°C (fig.6.9b). Even though the fire continued to grow, from this time on the temperature started to drop off slightly and ultimately settled at a level of about 430°C. Perhaps, this decrease was caused by the same factor as the one observed during firing II of the form p2KIV (fig.6.5b), when the accumulated embers and ashes had cut off the clay from high temperature of the open fire; as a result, the temperature of the clay which had had the time to rise considerably, started to drop off slightly.

Two hours into this firing episode the temperature started to grow again, on average, by 8.36°C (σ=7.09) every 15 minutes. The rate of increase was not stable and subject to substantial fluctuation.

The highest value, 516.8°C, was recorded during the last readout when the firing was at an end. It is quite likely that after the removal of the sensor temperature still continued to grow but definitely this was a very great increase as the fire had started to die down. The temperature diagram at point T2 was nearly identical as the diagram for point T1, but the temperature at bottom of the form was always lower. At first, the difference was on average 96.8°C (σ=28.05), and after reaching the value of about 400°C (at point T2) and about 460°C (at point T1), it gradually started to level off and dropped down to an average value of 38.04°C (σ=4.62). Similarly as on the surface of the clay, at its bottom the temperature initially increased quite rapidly but the rate of increase was not as high as in case of the value T1 and at first was around 85°C every 15 minutes, and subsequently, over the first one and a half hours, it dropped to around 20°C every 15 minutes. After reaching the value of 402.5°C, the temperature stated to drop off. The decrease in temperature at the bottom of the form occurred with a 15 minutes' delay as compared to the values obtained at point T1. After half an hour the value of the temperature started to grow again, but like in case of T1, this increase was not stable. The maximum value of 483°C, similarly as in case of T1, was noted during the last readout just before the end of the firing. After the sensors were removed the fire was left to burn itself out.

The next morning embers continued to smoulder inside the form but their quantity was much smaller than in forms p4KIV, or p14KIV which had been fired at the same time. Twelve hours after ending the firing the clay still retained a very high temperature–467°C at point T1, and 439°C at point T2.

After the second firing the zone of oxidised clay had grown but the centre still remained black. On its underside the clay remained dark brown and in some places, mostly near the centre of the form, it had started to turn black

Third firing

After temperature readouts were made the clay form was swept clean of all the embers and ashes and left to cool. The next firing was started the same day in the afternoon and lasted four hours. During the firing readouts of temperature were taken at point T1, even though the tunnel for inserting the sensor had fractured so that only the tip of the thermocouple was inserted in the clay and the rest of the wire was exposed from the top to the fire.

From the time of starting the firing the temperature started to rise rapidly (over the first half an hour there was an increase of more than 300°C) until reaching, after less than two hours, the maximum value of 655.2°C (fig.6.9c). After passing this mark the temperature dropped during 15 minutes by almost 90°C, to remain over the next two hours on more or less the same level, only with slight fluctuation caused by the nature of the fire itself. The average temperature at this time was 545.84°C (σ=20.45). At the time of the last readout the value was 520.8°C. After the end of the firing the fire was left for the night until it went out.

The next morning, after 14.5 hours, the embers continued to smoulder inside the form and the temperature readout at point T1 was 349.6°C. The readout at point T2 was 347.0°C. Both readouts indicated a very high level of heating of the form during the firing and a low rate of temperature reduction during the night. After the form was swept clean of the embers, the temperature of the clay started to drop off and half an hour later at point T1 its value was 231°C. This day the form p6KIV was not subjected to any more firings, and after the clay had cooled entirely the appearance of the upper and the bottom surface of the structure was recorded.

From the top the clay had turned non–uniform red–black. The red colour occupied over 50% of the surface but the black colour continued to dominate closer to the centre. On the underside, the black and dark brown colour which had dominated after the first two firings, had started to change colour and a part of the form next to the rim had turned light beige.

Fourth firing

During firing, which lasted eight hours, the temperature readouts were taken at point T1, with the same reservation as in case of the third firing.

Over the first half an hour the temperature rose to 380°C, after which the rate of increase dropped off observably and for the next two hours was on average 18.65°C (σ=8.64) every 15 minutes. After reaching a value of 530°C the temperature started to show a slight fluctuation and its increase became much slower, on average, 2.71°C (σ=4.43) every 15 minutes (fig.6.9d). This situation continued over the next two and a half hours of the firing until the temperature had reached the maximum value of 557.1°C. After this the temperature dropped off, and for the last three hours of the firing it continued to fluctuate between the value of 494.4°C and 554.4°C [average value of 522.3°C (σ=16.26)]. These fluctuations were caused by a shortage of firewood and the need to use small branches which produced an intensive but short–lived flame and raised the temperature of the fire for a short time. Once the firing ended and the embers had been swept from over the form, the temperature started to drop off very rapidly. Over the first 15 minutes it decreased by 240.3°C.

After the fourth firing the upper face of the clay form had turned red almost all over its surface except for a small area at centre some 10cm in diameter. On the underside, the form remained black and dark brown at centre but the oxidised zone, beige in colour, had increased in area as compared to the situation observed after the third firing. In the break, the clay was two–coloured, with a relatively well defined boundary between the red layer, which took in the upper portion of the structure and the rim, and a layer black and dark brown colour found on the underside of the cross–section at centre of the form (Pl.3.3). At the very centre of the form the break was brown on top and dark brown and black at bottom. Moving away from the centre, the slender black layer tapered off until it disappeared entirely in the area next to the rim. After being placed in water the clay did not revert to its original state.

Conclusion

A comparison made on a composite diagram of temperature curves from all the firing episodes shows that the temperature of the clay grew more rapidly with each firing and reached increasingly higher values (fig.6.10). Only in case of the fourth firing, despite its long duration, the attempt to reach the temperature obtained during the third firing was unsuccessful. It addition, we need to note that during both the second and the third firing episode a described earlier was observed, in which the temperature dropped off after the first two hours of firing and was only later followed by its gradual increase.

A composite diagram of the rate of temperature increase shows that the temperature of the clay grew with each successive firing following a similar pattern (fig.6.11).

Initially there was a rapid, usually a single (1 during 15 minutes) surge in temperature, higher with each successive firing. Subsequently, the rate of temperature increase declined visibly, after which it rose again. The two first peaks are visible on the diagram in all the firing episodes; only the third firing was characterised by a different appearance of the curve of temperature increase as the initial surge in temperature was longer (lasting half an hour) and the second peak almost did not happen. Even though, each time, the fire burns differently and it is not possible to create identical conditions within the fire, the diagrams of temperature increase show fluctuation at

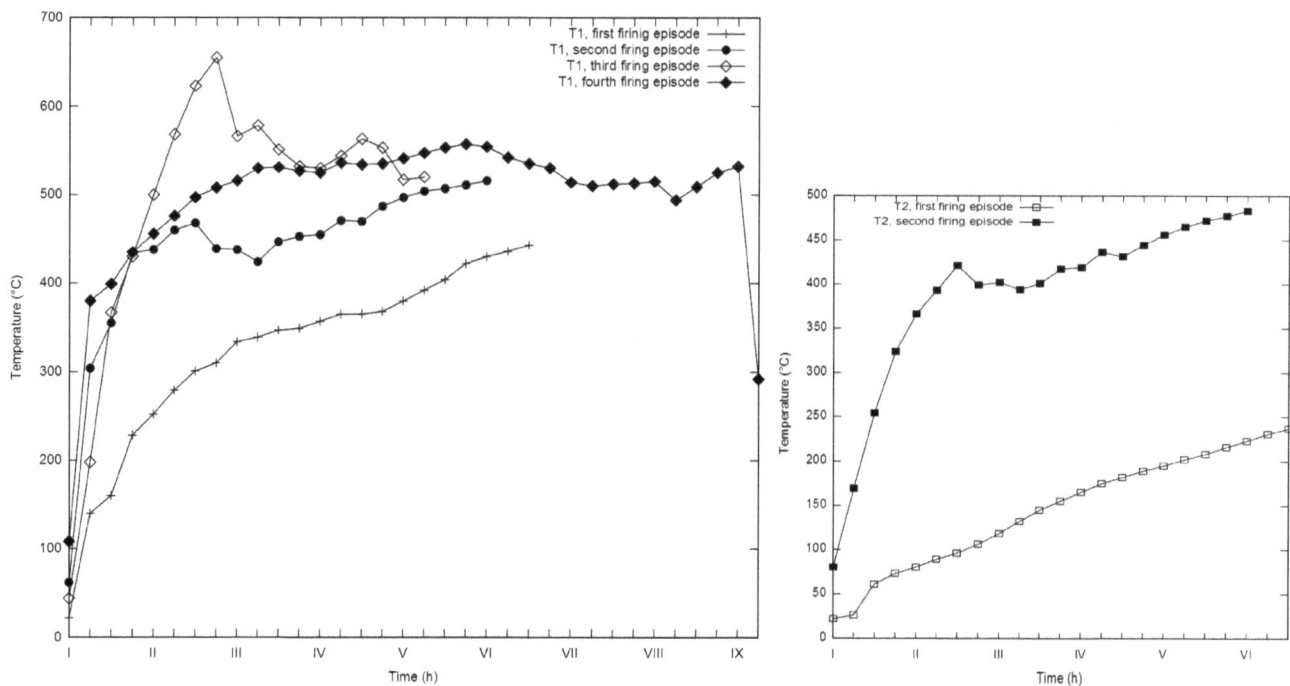

Fig. 6.10 A combined diagrams of temperature distribution in form p6KIV during all the firing episodes. On the left–T1–temperature just under the surface–not more than 5mm; on the right–T2–temperature on the bottom of the clay structure).

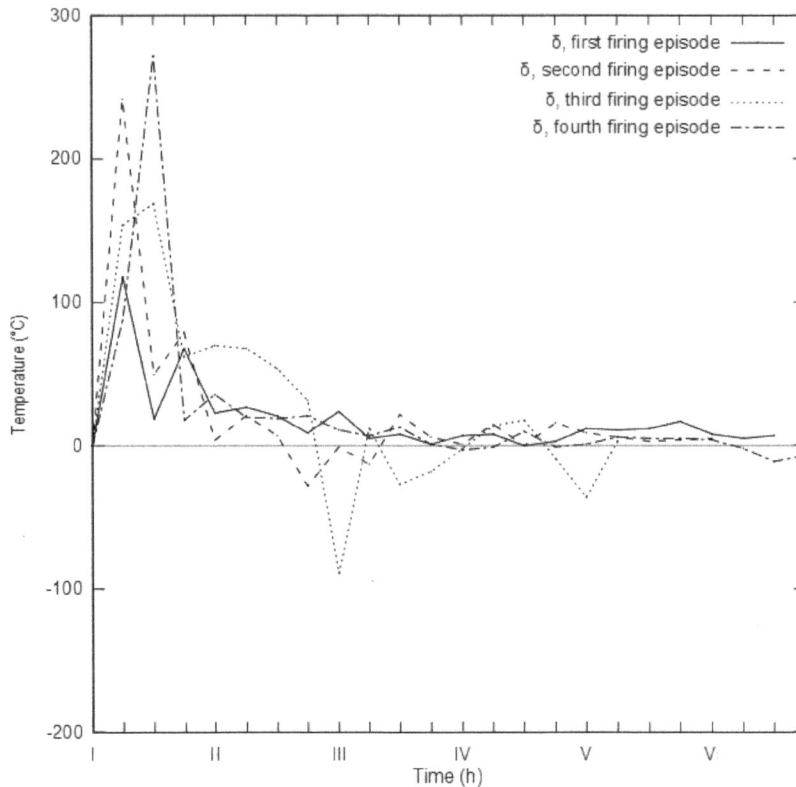

Fig. 6.11 A combined diagram of the rate of temperature increase in form p6KIV during all firing episodes.

almost the same moments; this suggests that these fluctuations are not linked to specific drops in temperature during specific firings, but have their causes in the thermic properties of the clay itself and the process of it becoming heated.

P7KIV

The purpose of building this form and firing it four times was to see what would be the impact on the colour of the clay on its underside from lifting the form from the ground after each firing to record its appearance. With this aim it was decided after building the form to leave it in the ground for the duration of all the firings and record its appearance only when the experiments were over.

P7KIV had a diameter of 35cm; the thickness of the clay was ca. 2cm. The rim of the form was 3cm over the level of its bottom. The fire was made each time over the form.

The first firing was started 48 hours after the form was built, when the clay had dried. The firing lasted eight hours. After four hours a temperature readout was made, at points T0/T1–on the surface of the clay–520°C, and within the clay form, at point T2, where the readout was 217.7°C. Because the first sensor was placed directly in the fire in order to be in contact with the clay, the first of these readouts may be overstated. After the end of the firing episode the fire was left to burn itself out. After the first firing the clay on the upper side of the form had turned black, except for small areas next to the rim.

The second firing started the next day in the morning after the form was swept clean of the ashes and the appearance of its upper side recorded. During the firing the embers were lifted and transferred to form p5KIV. This episode was brought to a close by the removal of all the embers and sweeping the form clean. After the second firing two–thirds of the upper surface of the clay had turned red. Only a circular area near the rim, descending towards the centre of the form, remained black. Perhaps this had been the centre of the fire as it was observed during firing that most forms remain black from the top at the very centre where the depth of the form is the greatest and tends to accumulate the largest quantity of embers and ashes, which perhaps, block the access of oxygen. In case of more shallow forms it is difficult to determine during firing where the form actually is, and the fire on many occasions is shifted in relation to the centre of the structure.

The third firing lasted around nine hours. During this time, as before, the embers were transferred in stages to form p5KIV and added to the fire of forms p11KIV and p12KIV. After nine hours of firing, when the fire started to go out, a temperature readout was made at point T0/T1. Its value was 479.5°C. The fire was left to go out and the embers and the ashes were swept out only the next day.

The clay had oxidised over a larger area. Only a small round area by the northern rim of the form remained black. The red colour was not limited to the upper surface but spread, where this could be observed, to the sides of the form, i.e. to the rim.

The last–fourth firing–lasted five hours. Similarly as in the case of the two preceding episodes forms p11KIV and p12KIV were placed in the fire. Embers were removed successively from p7KIV and added to p5KIV. After the end of the firing the form was swept clean of the accumulated ashes and embers and left to cool.

After four firing episodes the clay of the entire upper surface turned red in colour except for an area found at centre of the form which had become darker. A more detailed determination of the colour of the clay was not possible because its surface was covered by a slender layer of ashes. Only after the form was lifted from the ground a more detailed documentation became possible. The clay at bottom had turned black. Only a zone found about 3cm from the rims had become a non–uniform red (Pl.3.2). The boundary between the two zones was relatively well defined. In the break was visible a zone of oxidised clay found by the rims, and an area found at centre of the form which had turned black at bottom and dark brown at top (Pl.3.1). This was the colour which had been observed while recording the appearance of the form from the top. The thickness of the black layer at the very bottom was about 1.5cm.

The results of this experiment demonstrated that the lifting of the form from the ground after firing and its replacement causes the development of areas filled with air which facilitate oxidation of the clay. Leaving the clay in the ground for the duration of several firing episodes made it possible to establish that the clay at bottom became reduced even when exposed four times to the prolonged action of high temperatures.

P8KIV

This form, similarly as p9KIV, was meant to test a hypothesis formulated at the end of the third series of experiments, that the clay of a form which had been spread over with a layer of earth during firing would become oxidised on the underside. Because similar experiments had been made previously on forms which had been fired earlier at least once, it was decided to make a similar experiment on an unfired form. The plan of the experiment was to make the form p8KIV, make a fire over it without allowing it to dry and bury it and the fire with a layer of soil.

The diameter of the clay structure was 34cm, its thickness around 2cm. The depth of the form was 2–3cm. The same day, over the newly built form a fire was made which burnt for five hours. After this time it was buried under a large quantity of soil so that even no smoke issued from under it. In this state the form was left until the next day, when the soil was raked up and partly burnt fragments of wood were lifted and removed. Inside, the embers had already gone out. The form was lifted and both its sides documented. Both at top and bottom the clay had turned black and dark brown. In cross–section the form was entirely brown, and on one side next to the rim it was entirely black. Only a slender 1mm layer of clay on the surface of the rims on the side of the form had turned red. After the form was placed in water the clay in places where it was brown reverted to the original state, and in places where it had been fired black it only started to crumble.

P9KIV

The aim of building and firing this form was the same as in case of p8KIV. The difference was only that p9KIV was fired when dry. Additionally, after documenting the results of the experiments, a decision was taken to fire the form once again by building a fire over it in order to see whether the clay would become oxidised.

The form was relatively small (32cm in diameter) as compared to its substantial depth of 6cm. The thickness of the clay at bottom was 2–3cm. Below the clay structure was relatively friable soil.

The form was left to dry for 48 hours before it was subjected to the first firing of five and a half hours. The fire was built over the form. After four hours of firing a readout of the temperature of the clay was taken. With no tunnel to insert the sensor at point T1 it was decided to take this readout at point T0/T1, or, on the surface of the clay. The readouts brought the values of: 405.9°C, for T0/T1, and 317.6°C, for T2. After taking the readout the firing was continued for over an hour after which the form and the fire were buried under a thick layer of earth and left for the night. The next morning, before raking up the soil, the temperature of the clay was measured at point T0/T1 and a readout of 44.0°C obtained which meant that the embers had had time to die down during the night. After raking up the soil and lifting the incompletely burnt fragments of wood, the form was lifted from the ground to document the appearance of both its sides. The clay on the upper face had turned dark brown over almost the entire surface, except for small areas near the rim. On its underside the clay was entirely black. At centre, the colour of the clay had passed to dark brown colour .

After recording the form was placed back into the ground and subjected to a second firing which was to test whether the colour of the clay would change. The second firing lasted six hours and ended with the form being left for the night still filled with embers. The next morning, 19 hours after the end of the firing, the temperature of the clay was measured. At point T0/T1 the readout was 502.4°C, at point T2, it was 332.2°C. After taking the readouts the form was left buried under the embers. Five hours later, almost 24 hours after the end of the firing, the embers continued to smoulder within the form due to the relatively great depth of the form which helped it to sustain the heat.

After the second firing the form had an appearance analogous to that of other forms fired using open fire–at centre the clay had turned black in colour whereas at the rim it had oxidised and become red (Pl.3.4). At bottom the form had turned black except for small areas right next to the rim. In cross–section the clay was in some place of two, and even of three colours. At bottom was a black layer, at centre of the break–beige, and at top–red. The two–colour breaks were beige–black.

P10KIV

Building the form p10KIV had two basic objectives. The first was to test the behaviour during firing of a form of larger dimensions (over 50cm). The second objective was to test the behaviour (analogically to the experiment with firing p3KIV) of a form allowed to dry and then subjected to four brief firing episodes. Each time this was to be done by making a fire, heating the form as much as possible over two to three hours and finally raking out the fire and sweeping out the embers so that the clay would cool off. As in case of p3KIV, the aim of the experiment was to imitate the probable method of using this type of clay structures as places for roasting or heating food.

The finished form had a relatively large diameter of 50x56cm. Its depth was 4–5cm, thickness of the clay at bottom–about 2cm. The form was left to dry for 48 hours.

First firing

During the firing the temperature of the clay was measured at point T1/T2. The sensor was installed not at centre of the form, as it was too large, but about 10–15cm from the rim. Since the tunnel used to insert the thermocouple ran to the readout point from the bottom side of the form, an accurate placement of the sensor posed some problems and it was not always possible to accurately insert the tip of the thermocouple in the tunnel. In such a case it was inserted under the clay but, it seems, the thickness of the form at the readout point (ca.1cm) was small enough for this point to be referred to as T1/T2. The first firing lasted three hours. Initially the temperature increased slowly, only after 45 minutes of firing, when the temperature of the clay exceeded 150°C, there was in the space of 15 minutes a single surge of almost 200°C (fig.6.12a), possibly caused by the thermic conditions of the fire itself which, due to the large size of the form, did not cover the entire structure and burning at its centre gradually spread out. The temperature continued to rise for 15 minutes more, until it reached a maximum value of 394.3°C, after which it started to drop off. From this time on, over the next one and a half hours, the temperature continued at a stable level of 367.44°C (σ=3.93) until the end of the firing episode. The rapid drop in temperature which followed the achievement of the maximum temperature during the first hour of the firing was discussed in connection with the firing of forms p2KIV, p6KIV and could have been associated with the development of a layer of embers which cut off the clay from the directs source of heat, i.e. flames of the open fire.

When the firing was over the burning wood and embers were removed from over the form and it was swept clean of ashes. The form was left to cool but temperature readouts continued to be made. Initially (over the first 45 minutes), the rate of temperature decrease was on average 66.27°C (σ=10.47) every 15 minutes, but continued to level off steadily (fig.6.12a). Over the next 45 minutes its average value was 22.83°C (σ=4.98) for every 15 minutes. At the time of the last readout the temperature of the clay was 79.0°C.

After the firing ended the clay had turned non–uniform red at top, except for the rims and centre which had become darker in colour. On the surface there was a thin layer of ashes.

Second and third firing

These two firing episodes were performed one after the other with a two hours' break in between. For their entire duration a thermocouple had been inserted at point T1/T2 to record changes in temperature.

At the time when the fire was made the temperature of the clay started to rise rapidly until reaching the value of 450°C, after which, analogically to the situation observed during the first firing, it began to drop off (fig.6.12b). After a small fluctuation (of 20°C) the temperature of the clay started slowly but unsteadily to rise again at a rate of 36.9°C (σ=7.53) every 15 minutes, until reaching the maximum value of 541.7°C half an hour before the end of the firing episode. After the embers were swept out the temperature dropped abruptly. Initially, this drop was substantial and over the first 30 minutes occurred at a rate of 100°C every 15 minutes. But this rate of reduction became smaller and after two hours after the end of the firing and sweeping out the form had a value of 8°C every 15 minutes.

After the second firing the surface of the clay had become non–uniform red in colour, with a small patch of black ca. 10cm in diameter at centre of the form, and black discolorations by the eastern rim.

After two and a half hours after ending the firing when the temperature of the clay had dropped to 90.2°C, the third firing was started, which lasted two hours.

Immediately after the fire was made the temperature of the clay started to rise until it reached 375°C, when the rate of increase slowed down for about 15–30 minutes. After this time the temperature started to rise again with greater speed until reaching a maximum value of 473.8°C after which the firing was concluded. After the fire was raked out and the embers swept away the temperature started to drop off abruptly (fig.6.11b). Initially the decrease in temperature was 100°C for every 15 minutes but with time the rate of decrease grew smaller. An hour after ending the firing the decrease occurred at a rate of 9.4°C every 15 minutes and the temperature of the clay dropped to 162.5°C.

After the third firing the clay had turned a uniform red over the entire upper surface but the centre of the form

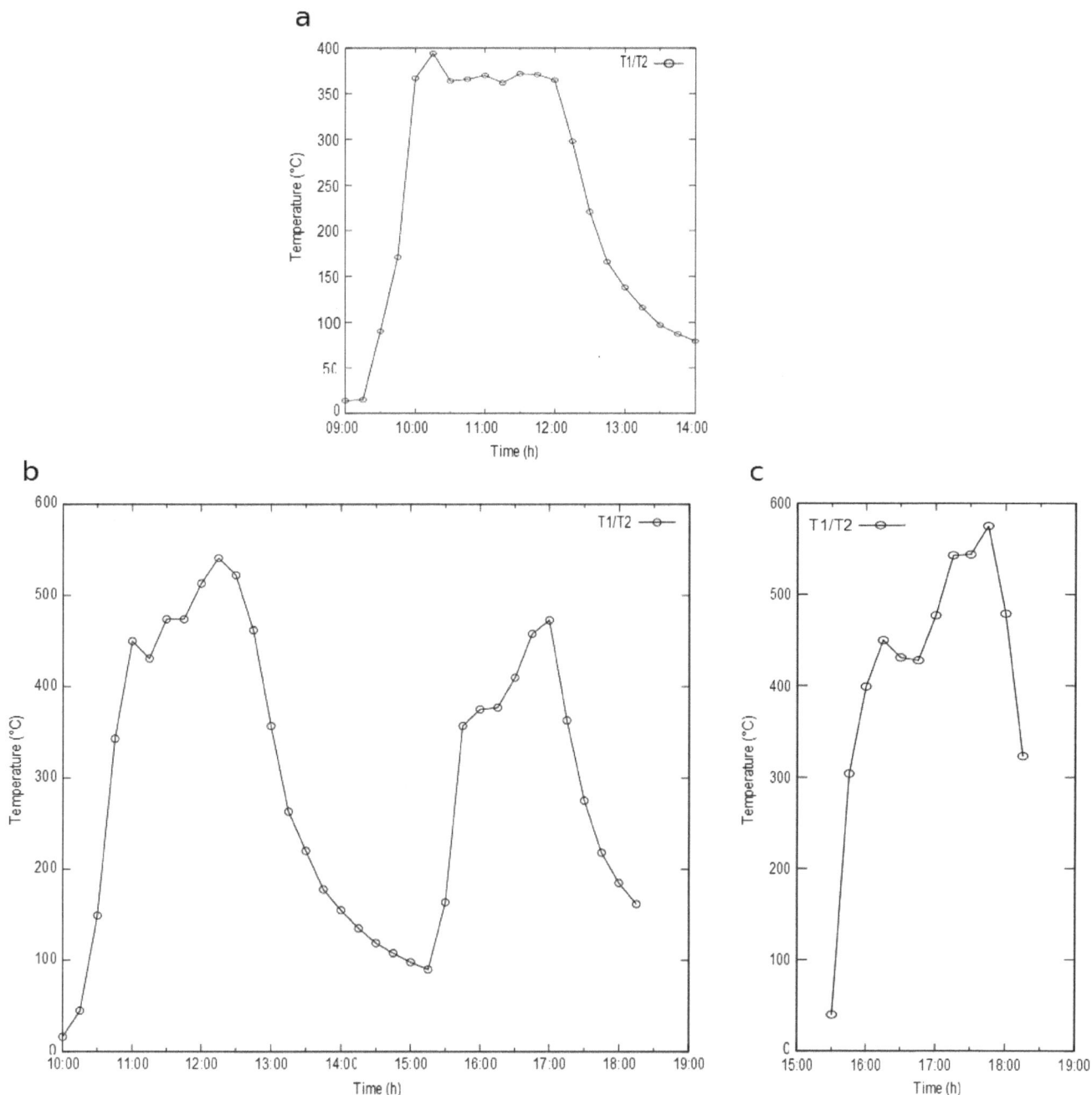

Fig. 6.12 Temperature distribution in form p10KIV during a) the first firing episode, b) the second firing episode, c) the third firing episode (T1/T2–temperature of the clay midway in the cross–section of the clay hearth).

remained black. The surface of the rims had turned a slightly different beige–red colour, possibly due to the lower temperature of the firing in these areas (the form had a larger diameter and was deep).

Fourth firing

The duration of the last firing was two and a half hours. During the firing and half an hour after its end the temperature of the clay at point T1/T2 was monitored. The temperature curve during this firing was similar as in earlier episodes. Initially, there was a rapid increase in temperature up to the value of 450.8°C, followed by a

slight drop. During the last hour of the firing there was a gradual though unstable increase in temperature to the maximum value of 575.7°C which was reached 15 minutes before the fire was raked out (fig.6.11c).

The clay after the fourth firing had become uniform red in colour. The black patch at centre had been reduced to only a darker discolouration with a diameter of ca. 5–7cm. From the bottom the clay after four firing episodes had become deep black in colour. The break of the form was in two colours–black from the bottom, and red on top. The black layer had a thickness of about 1/3 of the thickness of the break, except at centre of the form, where the break was non–uniform black in colour.

Conclusion

A composite diagram of the rate of temperature increase shows that with each firing the surge in temperature was more rapid (fig.6.13). It is also striking that these diagrams all have nearly the same curve; this suggests the similarity of the reaction by the clay during firing. A rapid increase in temperature was followed either by a drop off or a substantial slowing down of the rate of increase. Next, there was an observable increase in the rate of temperature rise which lasted until the end of the firing, which was followed by a rapid drop off in temperature.

With every consecutive firing the initial rate of temperature decrease was increasingly higher (fig.6.14). With each firing there was also an increase in the maximum temperature achieved and in the average values obtained during the firing. Only the third firing was different in this respect, but it must be noted that at this stage there was a shortage of wood and the fire had to be fed with smaller branches which are characterised by a low temperature of combustion.

P11KIV

This form was made, similarly as p12KIV, to test the behaviour of the clay from Klissoura in direct contact with open fire. With this aim a flat form with a small diameter of 23cm was built which once dry was subjected to three brief firing episodes by placing it directly in a fire. An attempt was made to speed up the drying process by placing the form near a fire which may caused some fissuring of the surface of the clay. During successive firing episodes the form each time was placed in a fire which was burning over p7KIV. The first firing lasted 3–4 hours. After this time the form was taken out and allowed to cool. After the first firing the surface of the clay had become black–grey–red on both sides.

The second firing lasted around three hours. The clay in places which had been black before, after the second firing had turned red–dark brown, whereas most of the surface remained non–uniform red colour with some black patches. The last firing was very brief. The form was placed in the fire for about two hours. During the firing the form became red–hot. After three firings the form had turned red over its entire surface. The black colour observed on one of the faces was the result of soot rather than of the process of oxidation or reduction of iron compounds. In cross–section the clay had turned red over the entire surface with small beige–coloured areas near the surface of the form.

P12KIV

The aim of making and firing this structure was similar as in case of form p11KIV described earlier, the only difference being that p12KIV was to be fired when still

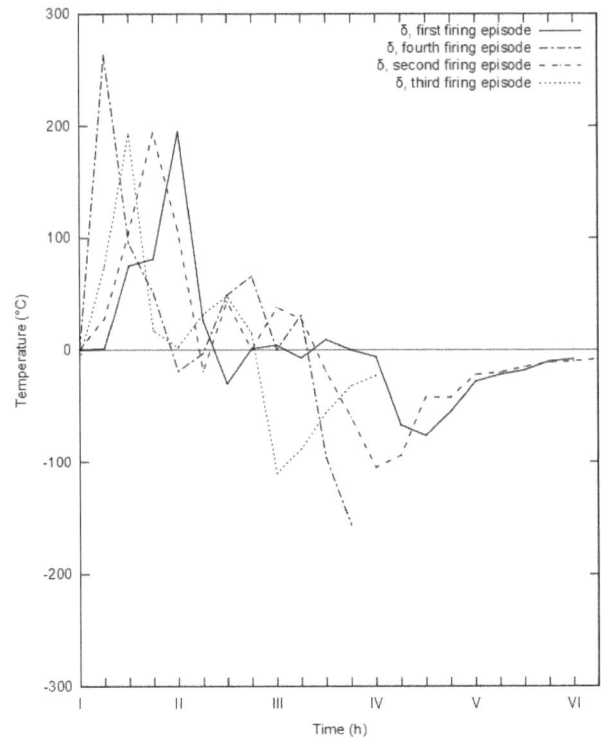

Fig. 6.13 A combined diagram of the rate of temperature increase in form p10KIV during all firing episodes.

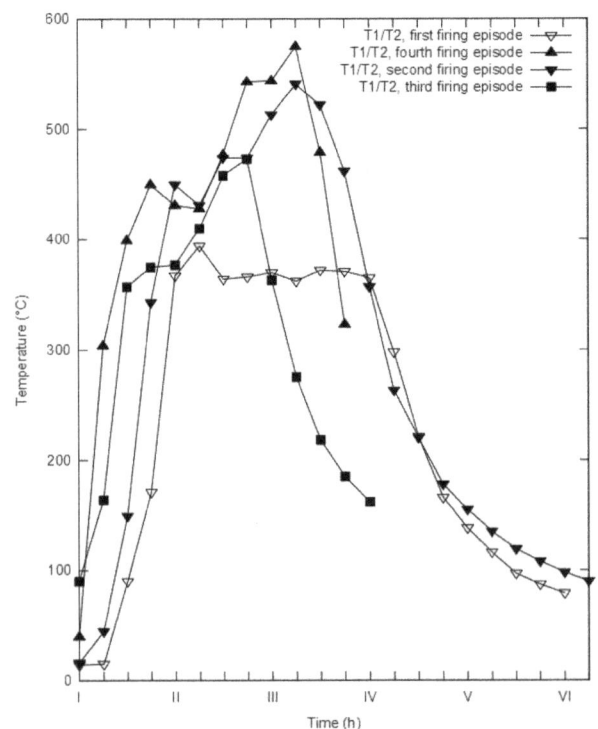

Fig. 6.14 A combined diagram of temperature distribution in form p10KIV during all the firing episodes (T1/T2–temperature of the clay midway in the cross–section of the clay hearth).

wet to test not only the appearance of the clay after firing directly in a fire, but also the behaviour of wet clay in contact with a very high temperature. The finished form was quite small–its diameter was 14cm. This flat "pancake" was at first placed close to a fire in order to have it dry a little and after an hour it was placed directly in a fire for about 3 hours. The form started to fissure on its surface right from the moment when it was placed closer to the fire but did not disintegrate even during firing. After being removed from the fire the surface of the form had turned non–uniform red and red–light brown. The second firing to which the form was subjected the next day was of a short duration but caused it to become red–hot. After the form was removed and allowed to cool, both its sides and cross–section were documented. The clay had remained non–uniform red–brown, and in some places, grey. In the break, there was an observable extensive zone of deep red colour and a small fragment of clay grey–brown passing to beige. Despite being fired when still wet the form had not disintegrated.

P13KIV

The aim of this experiment was to test other possible methods of making clay structures. P13KIV was produced over a number of days by pouring into a hollow in the ground having a diameter of around 30cm of water with a dissolved large amount of suspended clay. After each addition of the liquid the form was left to dry. This activity was repeated several times. Each time after the water and clay solution was added, sometime later the water became separated from the thick clayey substance and evaporated, leaving a very soft crust of clay. After the last similar treatment, the form was left to dry over 48 hours. During this time the clay started to crack and the cracks resembled hexagons which develop in drying mud. Ultimately the decision was taken to fire the form even though the clay still remained wet. The aim of the firing was to examine the appearance of the clay in cross–section and to see whether after firing it would develop into a compact layer or would fall apart. The firing lasted 5 hours. After this time the embers were swept out and it was allowed to cool. As it was not possible to lift the form from the ground it was decided to make a section through it. After this was done it was found that only a very thin (about 10–15mm) surface layer of the clay had been fired. After firing its colour had turned dark brown. The rest of the clay was not visible in section at all, perhaps it had been absorbed by the soil or become mixed with the sandy substrate. In a place where the fired form should have been was only a darker, wet and dark brown layer of the cave fill mixed with clay.

P14KIV

This form was built and fired in order to test alternative methods of making clay structures other than those used in earlier experiments. This was done by spreading the surface of a hollow dug in the ground with a layer of clay. Next, using wetted hands, the clay was worked and moulded into a form. This process took longer than usual but the obtained result could not be distinguished from forms built using other methods. The diameter of the structure was 36cm, thickness of its bottom–around 2cm. After the form was lifted it was found that some of its sides had a thickness of merely 7mm. The depth of the form was 3–4cm. This method of moulding a form was possible thanks to the characteristic lumpy texture of the clay which was used to build the forms during experiments. This clay, after extraction from the deposit, was moist but rather than sticking together it formed lumps which after wetting were easy to mould into the desired form.

The first firing of this form took place after it had become fully dry. A fire was built over the clay. The firing lasted less than seven hours. Two hours into the firing the temperature was measured at points T0/T1, on the surface of the form, and at T2, within the clay. At point T0/T1 the temperature of the clay was 342.8°C, at point T2–132.2°C. After the firing ended the fire was left for the night to go out. Over the night the embers continued to smoulder in the form (13 hours), and in the morning the temperature of the clay at points T0/T1 and T2 was, respectively, 446.6°C and 273.3°C. After the embers were removed and ashes swept out the form was lifted from the ground to record the appearance of the clay on its underside. In case of this experiment it was not the colour of the clay that mattered but its appearance and structure because of the non–typical method used to build the form. The colour of the clay at top was hard to determine which had to do with the settling on its surface of a thin layer of ashes. The clay at centre was in part black, and red near the margin. On the underside the form was entirely black but underneath a very thin layer of this colour could be seen a layer of dark brown. In the break at the rim the form was entirely dark brown. The texture of the clay on the underside was lumpy but the form had not become fragmented and could be lifted from the ground without much trouble.

The aim of the second firing was to see whether the dark brown layer which had appeared in the break of the form would disappear when the clay has been exposed to a high temperature. The fire burnt over the clay form for seven hours. After this time the fire was no longer fed and the embers left to go out.

The clay in case of the second firing had changed colour. On the upper surface it largely had become oxidised and turned red in colour. From below the form had become even more deep black in colour. The break was mostly in two colours: black at bottom, red at top (Pl.3.5). The boundary between the two layers in some areas was very clear, in others the transitional zone had a width of about 5mm and was either dark brown or beige in colour. The red–dark brown colour observed after the first firing had disappeared almost entirely.

P15KIV

The aim of making this form was to test the appearance in cross–section of a form fired only once when still wet.

The diameter of this structure was 35cm, its depth–2cm. The clay at bottom had a thickness of 3cm. It was built using method no. 2, or, by breaking apart a lump of clay on the bottom of a hole dug in the ground and moulding it into a flat "pancake". Once this had been done a fire was built over this form. Firing lasted over five hours. After this time the fire started to die out. The form and the embers were left for the night. The next morning the embers were still smouldering inside the form.

The clay was greatly fissured on the surface. The upper surface of the form had turned black except for small areas near the rim which had become oxidised. During lifting the form from the ground the clay broke into many small fragments because of the fissures within the clay. From below the clay was dark brown in colour, in cross–section it had turned a non–uniform black–brown. There were black traces of burnt out organic matter in the ceramic mass.

After a fragment of the clay form was placed in water the clay reverted in 30–50% to its original state, the remainder disintegrated into characteristic lumps except for a ca 3–5mm thick layer originating from the surface layer of the form.

Results from series IV of experiments–analysis

The comparison of temperature curves was made using difference of the average temperature because the duration of the firing episodes was not always the same and would have posed a problem when computing the temperature differences. The average temperature of a firing episode was computed without taking into account the first two readouts (30 minutes) since this is when the greatest surge in temperature occurred and these values amplified the standard deviation and lowered the average value. Moreover, the initial temperature of the clay at every firing was different, which substantially altered the average values.

First cycle

Involved in this cycle of experiments were:
P1KIV –fired wet –once –using embers,
P2KIV –fired wet –4 times –using fire,
P4KIV –fired wet –4 times –using embers,
P5KIV –fired dry –3 times –using embers,
P6KIV –fired dry –4 times –using fire.

During series IV of experiments not all of the planned experiments could be completed because form p1KIV, fired wet using embers, had broken after the first firing for whereas the clay structure p4KIV, fired in similar conditions (wet, using embers), we do not have an unbroken diagram of the temperature of the clay during the firing episodes.

Given this state of affairs we have at our disposal diagrams of temperature for a single firing episode with p1KIV, four firing episodes with p2KIV, three firing episodes with p5KIV and four firing episode with p6KIV.

1. Temperature. A comparison of temperature curve readouts from the first firing (fig.6.15a) shows that the value of readouts taken at point T2, or, on the underside of the form, are almost identical for firing episodes using embers and open fire with forms allowed to dry before firing (p5KIV, p6KIV). Even though the temperature of the upper layers of the clay differs substantially and the diagram for each form has a different curve, the lower layers of the clay heated at the same rate and reached nearly identical values. Additionally, a comparison of temperature diagrams obtained from firing episodes with wet forms (p2IV, p1KIV) shows that the tendency during firing wet clay structures using an open fire is the same as in the case of the two just described, and only the range of temperature values obtained is lower. The difference between the average temperatures of the clay at point T2 during firing with an open fire of a dried form (p6KIV), and of a wet form (p2KIV), was 28.02°C in favour of the dried form. This means that the clay fired when still wet using an open fire (p2KIV) heats in the same way as a form fired after drying but does not reach the same temperatures.

The lowest temperature values are achieved by clay fired when still using embers. The difference of average temperature of clay in a dried form (p5KIV) as compared to a wet form (p1KIV) was 86.07°C. The initial temperature increment in p1KIV occurred at the same rate as in the three cases already described (p2KIV, p5KIV–T2, p6KIV–T2) but later the rate of increase was arrested, caused by the continued presence of water within the clay. Water starts to evaporate when clay is heated to a temperature of ca. 100°C. After passing this boundary the temperature starts to grow. In case of firing wet clay forms using embers it is difficult to achieve the temperature of evaporation of the clay which causes the water to remain in the form.

The temperature of the surface of the clay in firing episodes where an open fire was made was on average higher by 69.82°C than temperature of the surface of the clay in a form fired using embers (p6KIV/T1–p5KIV/T1). The difference between the surface of the clay and the underside of the clay form in a form fired after drying using an open fire (p6KIV) was on average 189.57°C In a form fired using embers (p5KIV) the respective value was 102.95°C.

During consecutive firing episodes the average temperature of the clay grew and the initial rate of increase became increasingly higher. Starting from the second firing it no longer mattered whether the form had been fired wet or when dry, as the water trapped within the spaces between the clay particles (Rice, 2005) had had time to evaporate during the first firing. A comparison of temperature diagrams from all second firing episodes shows that the lowest temperature prevailed during firing episodes where embers were used (fig.6.15b). The highest temperature (240°C) during the first heating of the clay was achieved by a form fired with

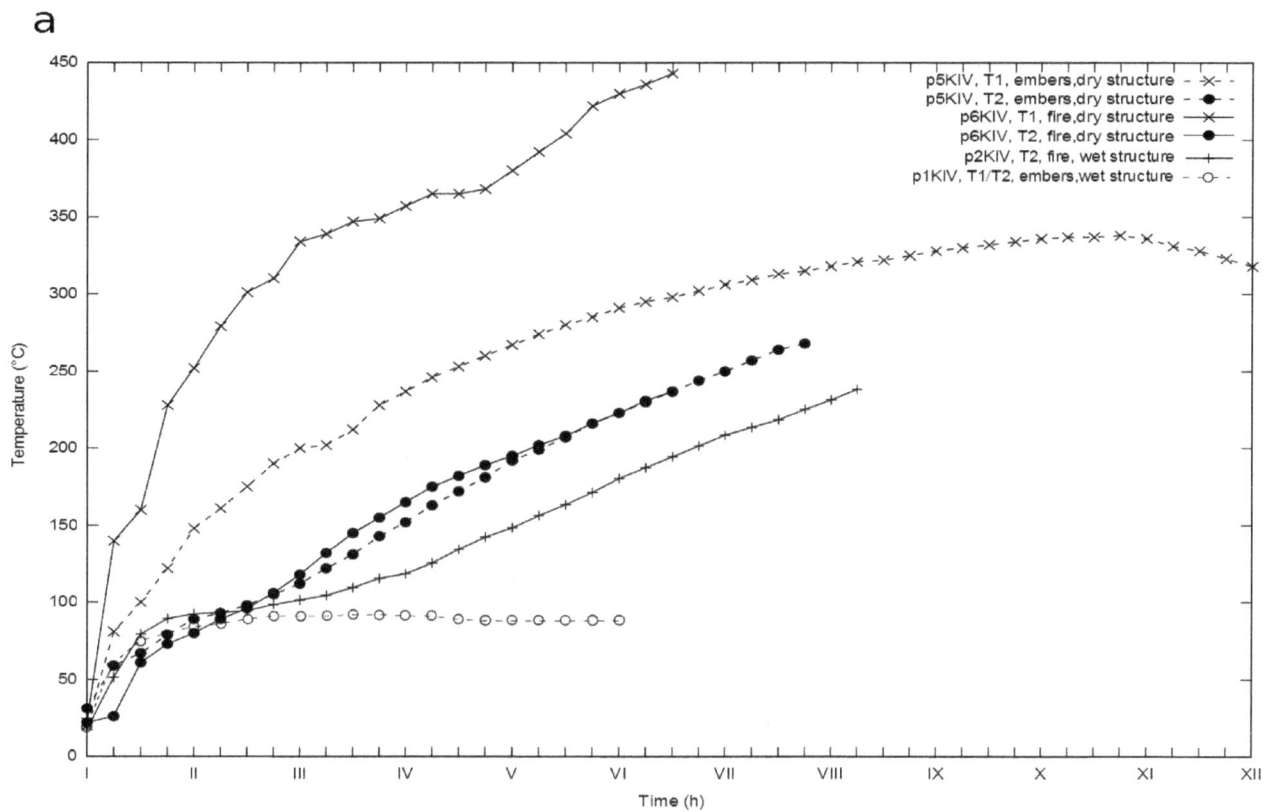

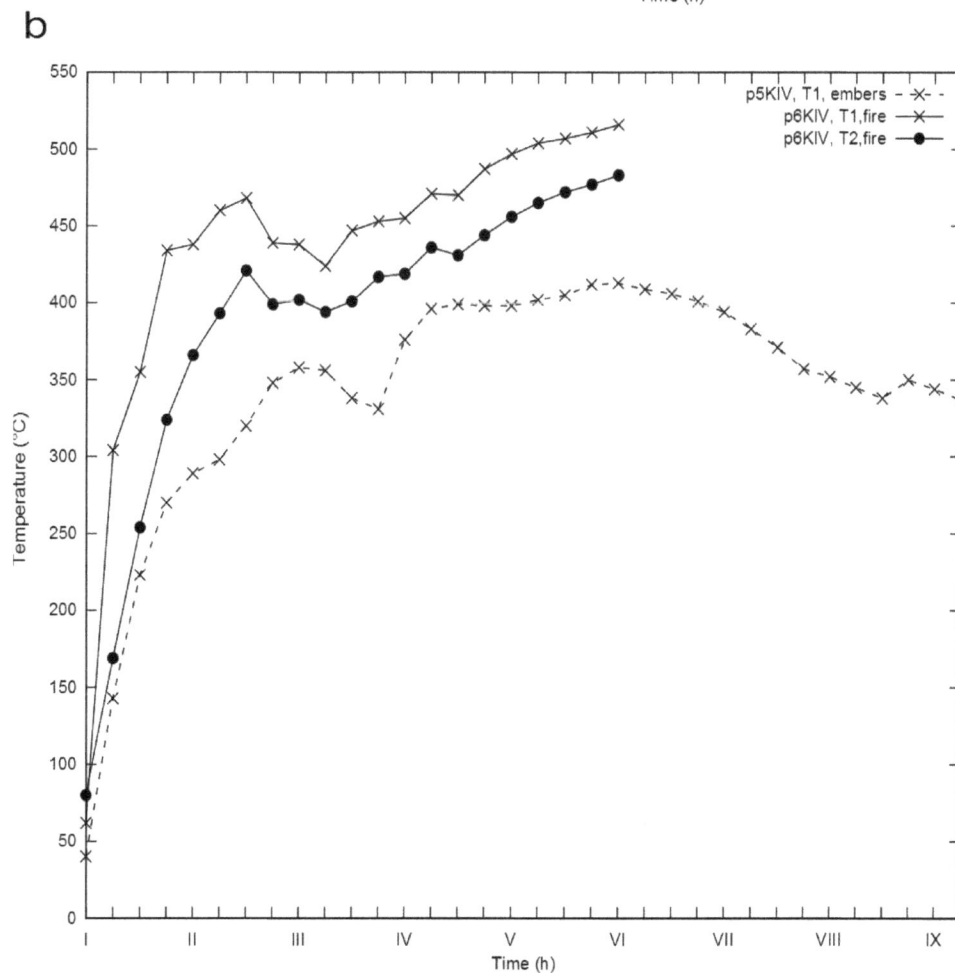

Fig. 6.15 A combined diagram of temperature distribution of forms p1KIV, p2KIV, p5KIV and p6KIV during a) the first firing; b) the second firing (T1–temperature just under the surface–not more than 5mm; T1/T2–temperature of the clay midway in the cross–section of the clay heart; T2–temperature on the bottom of the clay structure).

an open fire which, before the fire was made, had not yet lost the heat obtained during the first firing.

A comparison of the rate of temperature increment shows that even though form p2KIV had achieved the highest temperature its rate of temperature increase had been the same as in other firing episodes measured at point T2. Despite the initial heated condition of this form the rate of temperature increase remains the same. What is altered is only the higher range of temperatures obtained when firing this particular form.

The same initial rate of temperature increase was observed both in the clay of p5KIV at point T1 (firing using embers), as p6KIV, at point T2, and p2KIV, at point T1/T2 (both fired using open fire). This increment involved an initial increase of temperature by about 100°C followed by a slow levelling off of the rate of temperature increase. The conclusion from this is that the clay on a surface fired with embers heats analogically as clay found at bottom of a form during a firing where an open fire is used. A different diagram of the rate of temperature increase was obtained only for the temperature of clay on the surface of a form fired with an open fire. The initial surge in temperature is very high, about 250°C. Next, the rate of increase levels off. Fluctuation in the rate of temperature increase which follows the initial surge of temperature is associated with the individual progress of the firing, individual in case of every experiment.

The differences in average temperature obtained for the firing episodes are not high. Between the surface and bottom layer of the clay in p6KIV the difference is 48.5°C (during the first firing the value was 189.57°C), whereas the difference in temperature between clay fired using embers and an open fire (p2KIV/T1–p5KIV/T1) this value is 126.6°C. The difference of temperature readout taken at same point in two forms fired using an open fire is 7.57°C.

In case of the two last clay forms the author has only incomplete data because not all the forms had been subjected to a fourth firing. Consequently, the conclusions drawn from the composite diagrams are limited.

A comparison of temperature diagrams from the third and fourth firing shows that the lowest values are those obtained during firing where embers were used. In case of firing using an open fire the average temperature values are higher by 140°C (p2KIV/T2–p5KIV/T2). The difference in the average temperature at points T1 and T2 (p6KIV/T1–p2KIV/T2) is one of 132.12°C in case of the third firing, and 130.79°C in case of the fourth. Nevertheless it must be noted that these calculations correspond to different clay forms and not to differences in temperature of the clay in one and the same form.

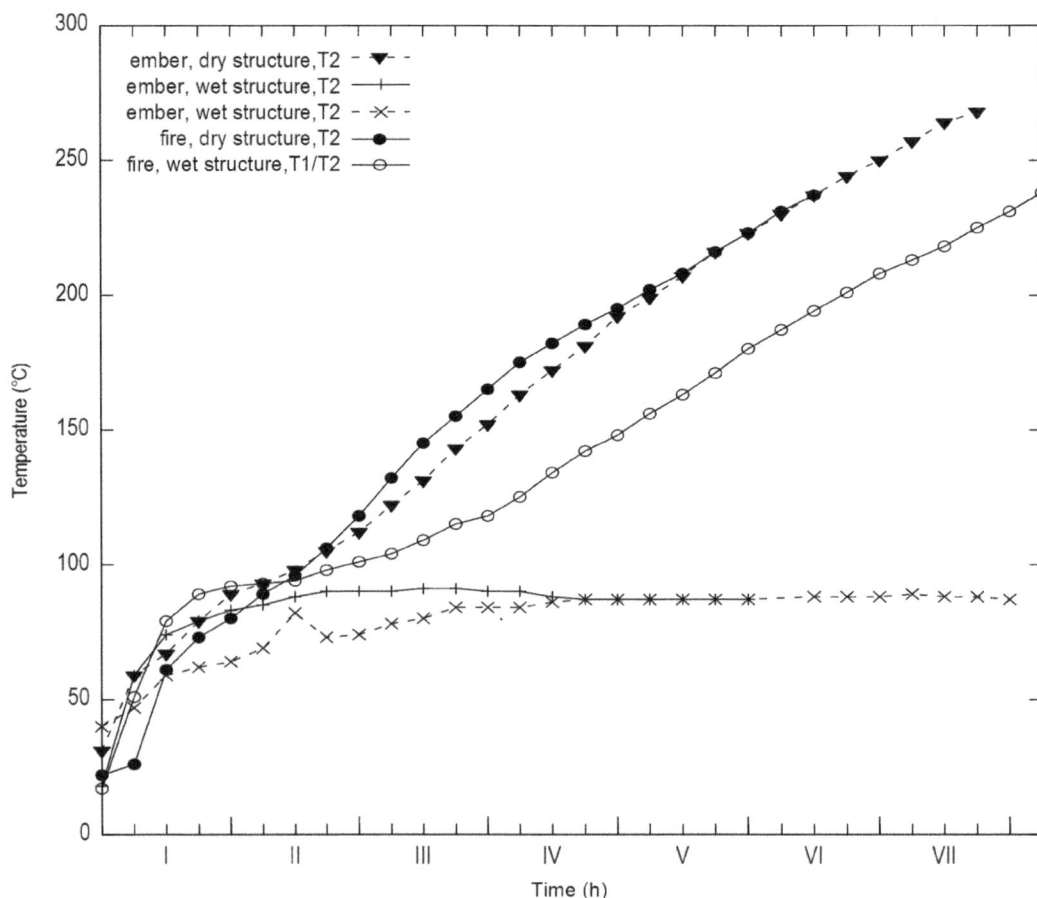

Fig. 6.16 A combined diagram of temperature distribution of forms fired by embers and fire.

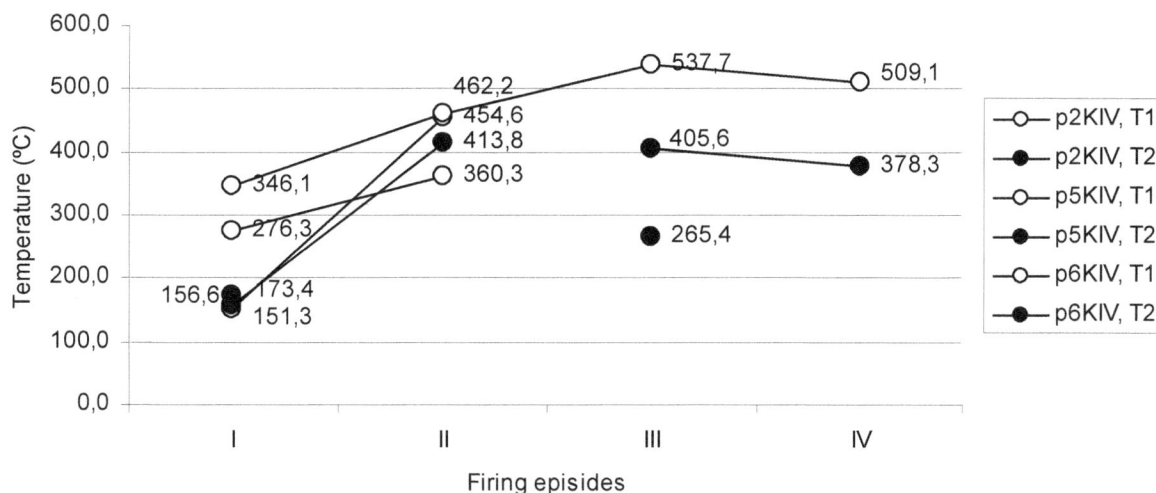

Fig. 6.17 A comparison of the average temperature during four firing episodes.

Finally to wrap up the analysis of the temperature obtained during different firing episodes we have to conclude that the highest temperature was obtained for clay fired when dry using an open fire (p6KIV). The maximum temperature value of clay measured at point T1 was 655.2°C (third firing), at point T2–483°C (second firing). Later, the value T2 was not measured so it is unclear what was the maximum value achieved during the firing episodes. Slightly lower temperatures were obtained for clay fired wet using an open fire. The maximum temperature at point T1/T2 was 484.8°C. Whereas the temperature of the clay in p6KIV starting from the second firing regularly exceeded 500°C, in case of p2KIV the temperature was always below 500°C. Let it be noted nevertheless that the temperature readout for p2KIV had been made inside the clay (ca. 1cm below the surface) whereas for p6KIV it had been taken from a smaller depth (ca. 0.5cm below the surface)

Firing using embers caused the clay to heat to a much lesser extent. In case of firing dried clay forms the clay reached during the second firing a maximum recorded temperature of 413.3°C (T1), and 313.8°C (T2). The lowest temperature value was recorded when firing a wet form using embers. Unfortunately, in this case we have no unbroken record of temperature, only isolated readouts made during the firing, but when compared against other firing episodes they show that the clay was much slower to heat. During the second firing, after 5 hours after being placed in the embers, the recorded temperature values were: 285°C (for T1) and 185.5°C (T2); (cf., p5KIV, second firing, after 5 hours–413.3°C, for–T1). The maximum value recorded for p4KIV at T1 was 348.3°C–a readout made in the morning 18 hours after the last replenishing of the embers, and T2–280.5°C–5 hours after starting the third firing.

Even repeated firing of a form does not cause an increase in temperature higher than 650°C, which temperature seems to be the upper limit for forms fired using an open fire.

2. Colour of the clay. As regards change in the colour of the clay induced by firing it is possible to observe some regularities. After the first firing the clay turned black, both on the upper surface and on the underside. Only the areas next to the rim underwent oxidation and turned red in colour. In the course of successive firing the black zone at centre of the clay form became smaller and gave way to an area of oxidised clay. The colour of the form on its underside was dependent to a great extent from the method of firing and consequently, presumably also the temperature of firing. Forms fired after being allowed to dry, whether using embers or an open fire, turned black on their underside. Successive firing episodes caused either an expansion of the black coloured surfaces, if prior to firing the surface had been dark brown–black, or a gradual oxidation of the clay and the change of colour to beige, if after an earlier firing episode the clay had turned black. The sequence of the colour change was therefore as follows: first, the clay turned brown/dark brown, next, it became black on its underside only to become oxidised with time, and starting from the rim, to turn beige or red. However, most often the central part of the underside of the form remained black. After firing in temperatures higher than 400°C the form developed a two–coloured cross–section–red at top, black at bottom.

When wet forms were fired using embers it was possible to observe the appearance of clay developed in response to lower temperatures. In these cases the form developed a brown cross–section, and with time, turned black on its underside or at centre of the upper surface. Such clay, after being placed in water reverted to its original state and became pliable again, but not always over its entire surface (p4KIV, p1KIV, p15KIV). An interesting result was obtained from the repeated firing, using embers, of the wet form p4KIV. As mentioned earlier, the temperatures to which this form was heated most likely were not higher than 400°C. The clay after the fourth firing became a uniform dark–red–brown, with small patches of black. This colour corresponds to a great extent to the one observed on prehistoric "clay hearths"

49

from Klissoura. At the same time, experiments with a single firing of two wet forms by spreading them with a layer of embers (p1KIV and p15KIV) demonstrated how different results may be obtained from this method of firing without changing the basic coefficients we can regulate. One of the forms (p1KIV) after firing was entirely brown and the clay remained fully pliable after being placed in water. In case of the second form (p15KIV) the firing caused a change of colour to black, and in cross–section it had become a non–uniform black–brown. The clay after being placed in water reverted to its original state only in 30–50% of its volume, the remainder disintegrated into non–pliable lumps. It seems that the temperature of the clay had been in this case higher but the person making the experiment had had no control over this whatsoever.

The results of experimentation show that the black colour with each firing became reduced in area but it is difficult to say to what extent this was due to increased oxygen inflow to the underside of the form caused by the form being lifted from the ground and put back again or whether this is a natural process which occurs independently of this factor. To test the hypothesis about the impact of the removal of the form on colour change of the underside of the clay structure, form p7KIV was fired. The result of four firing episodes is discussed above. The underside of the form had turned an unprecedented colour: at centre–deep black–not obtained during any of the other experiments. A circular black patch with a diameter of around 30cm surrounded by oxidised clay next to the rims. On its surface the form was also nearly entirely red except for a small black spot at centre of the form. The cross–section of the form was definitely black–red, with a slender black layer at bottom which tapered off moving away from the centre of the form, suggesting that with successive firings the clay in these places would also have become oxidised, although this is not certain. On the one hand therefore, the form which had not been lifted after each firing was more deep black in colour on its underside, on the other, it also had developed on its lower surface an oxidised zone of a form not observed on other clay hearths. This may be connected to the fact that after the forms had been recorded and placed back in the ground their rims were spread over with earth and ashes to keep out the air. Presumably therefore, the form, poorly fitted to the substrate, had had underneath an area with pockets of air and this facilitated oxidation from below, and, at the same time, the burying of the rims had cut off access of oxygen to this part of the form.

Interesting findings as regards the colour of the clay were obtained from the firing of p2KIV. This form was fired for the first time when still wet after being placed over an experimental clay hearth left in the ground after the 2006 series. Whereas the colour of the clay after this first firing resembled the result of other such episodes: the clay on top was nearly black all over for an area near the rim which had become oxidised, after the second firing the entire form had turned uniform bright red in the entire cross–section and this did not change after two further firings. It is difficult to offer a more specific reason for

such a change in colour. Although the seriously fissured condition of the form may have increased oxygen access why would this not have had impact on oxidation of other forms fired when still wet? Perhaps the combination of the factor of firing with open fire of a wet form was significant but we need to note that after the first firing the form had an altogether different appearance. One more factor could be relevant in attempting to interpret this development. The second firing had started at a time when the form was still quite hot after the first firing. At the time when a new fire was made over the form the temperature of the clay was 240°C. This factor contributed to a rapid increase in temperature which, even though it proceeded according to a pattern seen during other firing episodes (p5KIV, p6KIV), it had caused the temperature of the firing to become very high (average value–454.6°C).

Second cycle

In case of this cycle of experiments it was possible to carry them out in full, obtaining additional information in the form of temperature readouts from all the firing episodes of one of the forms (p10KIV).

Involved in this cycle of experiments were:
p3KIV –fired wet –5 times, –using an open fire
                –short duration,
p10KIV –fired dry –4 times.–using an open fire
                –short duration.

Average temperatures obtained during the firing episodes were high. During the first firing they were higher than during the first firing of the form p6KIV. The average value of the readout made at point T2 was 326.89°C whereas the maximum value during the same firing episode was 394.3°C (for p6KIV, the respective values were as follows: average–156.58°C, maximum–237.6°C). However it must be noted that the form p10KIV was relatively thin, with a thickness at the point where temperature readout of less than 1.5cm; for this reason the temperature readout at point T2 was closer to the value obtained at T1 during the first firing of p6KIV (three hours into this firing episode–average–296.42°C, maximum value–365.1°C).

During successive firing episodes the average temperature values were comparable to the values obtained for analogous firings of p6KIV. In the second firing the average temperature was 436.22°C (for p6KIV/T1–462.17°C, for p6KIV/T2–413.77°C). In the third firing the average temperature of the clay was 408.72°C (p6KIV/T1–537.72°C) and in the fourth–481.09°C (p6KIV/T1–509.11°C).

The temperature results obtained while firing p10KIV cannot be compared easily with those described earlier because in case of experiments performed as part of the second cycle the aim of the firing episode was to heat the form as quickly as possible to the highest possible temperature and then to sweep it clean. Therefore, the fire burning over the form was always larger than the one burnt over other forms. An additional factor which possibly influenced the method of firing and thermic condition of the clay was that the form p10KIV had quite a large diameter of 50x56cm.

In case of firing episodes with p10KIV, and also of some of the firing episode with p2KIV and p6KIV, there is an observable initial abrupt increase in temperature followed by its decline by several score degrees. As a rule this took place about and hour and a half into the firing. Observing the fire carefully one may try to explain this development by the fact of successive accumulation of the embers at bottom of the form. Initially, when the fire had just been made the heat generated by it could directly act on the clay raising its temperature but once the embers and ash had started to collect on the surface of the form, they cut of the clay from the direct source of heat and themselves became a source of lower heat, with a temperature around 200°C.

Short–lived intensive firing episodes did not affect colour change in the clay as compared to firing episodes of a longer duration. A form fired when wet (p3KIV), after five firings turned brown in colour and on the underside became black–brown. By its appearance it resembled other forms fired wet (p4KIV, p14KIV, p15KIV). The second form fired when dry (p10KIV) developed after firing a break of two colours like other forms fired when already dry–p7KIV, or p6KIV.

Third cycle

The firing of two forms as part of the third cycle of experiments demonstrated that even firing using an open fire with full access of oxygen leads to the development of a non–uniform colour on the surface of the form and the clay turns red–dark grey on its surface and in cross–section is almost entirely red in colour. Results of these experiments also demonstrated the durability and fine ceramic properties of the clay from Klissoura. Forms built of this material, even if fired when still wet, do not disintegrate, only become fissured but this does not lead to their disintegration. The character of firing: dry or wet, does not influence the colour of the clay.

Fourth cycle

The aim of this cycle, as mentioned earlier, was to test a hypothesis formulated in response to the results from the third series of experiments. These had shown that the burying of a form and the fire burning over it under a layer of soil and consequently, cutting off the access of oxygen, unexpectedly, causes oxidation of the clay at bottom of the form and at the same time, a strong reduction of the clay within, which led to the development of a blue–grey colour in the cross–section (p1RIII). However, experiments made at Vadastra had involved forms which had been fired earlier and thus it was not certain whether the reduction of the clay had been the effect of repeated firing or of the burying of the form under a layer of soil. The fourth cycle of experiments was intended to answer this question by firing only once two forms (one allowed to dry–p9KIV,

one when still wet–p8KIV) and finally burying them under a layer of soil.

Involved in this cycle were:
P8KIV –fired wet –once –using an open fire
            –buried under a layer of earth,
P9KIV –fired dry –2 times –using an open fire
            –buried under a layer of earth.

The results of experiments demonstrated that after being fired wet and buried under a layer of soil the clay became almost fully reduced and turned black, both on the upper surface and the underside, in cross–section–dark brown. The structure fired dry had an identical appearance, was black from the bottom and dark brown in cross–section.

When form p9KIV was fired the second time by making a fire over it, the upper part of the clay became oxidised and developed a cross–section of two colours–red from the top, and black at bottom.

These experiments show that, very likely, the oxidation which occurred after the form was buried under a layer of earth as part of series III of experiments, had been caused by repeated firing and not by the burying of the form with earth. At the same time, it cannot be excluded that the burying of the form could have influenced the extent of oxidation of previously fired forms, but in case of forms fired for the first time the clay behaves in a predictable manner and becomes reduced, turning a distinctive black colour. The blue–grey colour of the cross–section of form (p1RIII) presumably was associated with a different raw material used to make the form. In case of *terra rosa* clay none of the cross–sections had blue–grey colour.

At the same time, experiments demonstrated that reduction even of a large portion of a clay form may, during successive firing in oxygen rich conditions, be followed by oxidation of iron compounds and development of red colour.

Fifth cycle

The fifth cycle of experiments remained an open project at the planning stage because its aim was to test alternative methods of making clay forms meant to improve their ergonomics or change the appearance of the clay forms. As part of this cycle two experiments were performed which involved building and firing forms p13KIV and p14KIV.

The clay form p13KIV after firing was nothing like the clay structures found in cave Klissoura because the clay did not form a layer at all and had been absorbed by the surrounding soil and had not become fired.

Results of the experiment with p14KIV seem much more interesting because it was found that the appearance of the form after it was created did not differ from the appearance of forms built using other methods. At the same time, we have to stress that this method of making a clay form is feasible only when the clay is already moist and does not form rock hard dry lumps. In this case, placed in a hollow and moulded using wet hands it may be worked into a uniform mass. On its underside the form retains a grainy texture (its lumps have not bonded), but the form is still quite compact as a whole and does not disintegrate.

CHAPTER 7

RESULTS

General remarks

The deeper the clay structure was the longer the embers continued to smoulder inside the form when left. In clay form p4KIV and p9KIV during one of the experiments embers continued to smoulder 24 hours after the last replenishing of wood. On the basis of conducted experiments it can be concluded that the most preferable size of clay structures for storing smouldering embers would be ca. 30cm in diameter and 5–10cm in depth.

Moulding the clay hearth by battering the flattened ball of clay into the required shape by fist seems to be most effective. On one hand the clay structures moulded this way are the most fracture resistant. On the other hand it does not make it possible to control the thickness of the experimental clay hearth while it is being modelled. At the same time, this method is consistent with archaeological evidence since after forming the hearths using the first method the underside of the clay hearth shows traces of plastering together of several clay rounds, something which was not observed on the forms from Klissoura.

Results: thermal properties

On the basis of the conducted experiments it may be concluded that predictably among four tested methods of firing (in wet conditions using embers, in wet conditions using direct fire, in dry conditions using embers, in dry conditions using direct fire) less time was needed for the clay to heat in a dried clay hearth fired using fire made directly over it. In such case the clay within two hours reaches a temperature of ca. 300°C. During a firing episode of several hours the clay heats to a temperature of ca. 400°C–500°C.

A dried clay hearth fired using embers and a clay hearth fired when still wet using direct fire heat heats at a similar rate whereas the values measured at point T2, or underneath the clay hearth are nearly identical when firing dried forms both with embers and with fire (fig.7.1.b). Even though the temperature of the surface layers of the clay differs substantially and the diagrams for each of these forms are different, the lower layers of the clay heat at the same rate to an almost identical temperature.

The slowest to heat is the clay in a clay hearth fired when still wet using embers. In this latter case the water usually has not time to evaporate from the form and the clay stays wet. The maximum temperature of clay obtained during firing with embers of a wet form was: 300°C at the surface of the clay hearth and 280°C on its underside.

During experiments there was observed the occurrence of substantial differences in temperature depending on the readout point. The clay in a clay hearth heats unevenly as it is subjected to the action of high temperature only from the top. This fact and low thermal conductivity of the clay cause the layers found lower down to heat to temperatures lower by between 100°C and 200°C than the layer of clay in direct contact with the fire (fig.7.1.a). During firing the clay at the bottom of the clay hearth is subjected to continuous heating and conceivably if the firing lasted long enough (perhaps even for more than 24 hours) then the temperature of the clay in the entire clay hearth might have become uniform.

Even the layer of clay in direct contact with fire never develops a temperature equal to that of the fire itself but as a rule is lower by ca. 280°C. thus while the temperature of the fire is within the range of 700–900°C, the temperature of the surface layers of the clay hearth is 550–650°C, of bottom layers in direct contact with the ground–300–400°C. The similar results were obtained by March, Muhieddine and Canot while measuring the temperature distribution of a ground below fireplace (2010, fig.3).

A clay hearth fired when still wet is slower to heat and during a firing episode of several hours it heats to a maximum temperature of ca. 300°C. Water starts to evaporate from the clay when the temperature of ca. 100°C has been reached. Subsequent to this the temperature of the clay starts to increase gradually. In case of firing a wet clay hearth using embers it is hard to reach the temperature at which the clay starts to steam, which causes the water to remain in the clay hearth (fig.7.1.a).

However, clay hearths fired when still wet using direct fire tended to crack substantially as a result of being subjected to very high temperature. Water evaporating from the clay rapidly escaped to the surface and caused the ceramic mass to explode. (Rice, 2005). At the same time it is worth noting that the degree of cracking of *terra rosa* clay as a result of firing a wet clay hearth with direct fire is much smaller than in procedures using postglacial clay.

Terra rosa clays are characterised by sufficiently fine quality that, unlike postglacial clays, not only permit uncontrolled process of drying but also can be fired when wet without danger of cracking up altogether. This could have been a factor favourable for the idea of using clay hearths and for the survival of the tradition of building this type of clay hearths for a very long time.

In the course of successive firing processes the clay heats the same way irrespective of whether the clay hearth was fired for the first time when still wet or after drying. With each successive firing the time needed for the clay to achieve a maximum temperature becomes shorter (fig.6.13). After achieving the value around 500–600°C the temperature of the clay stabilises and is not subject to further temperature increase.

a

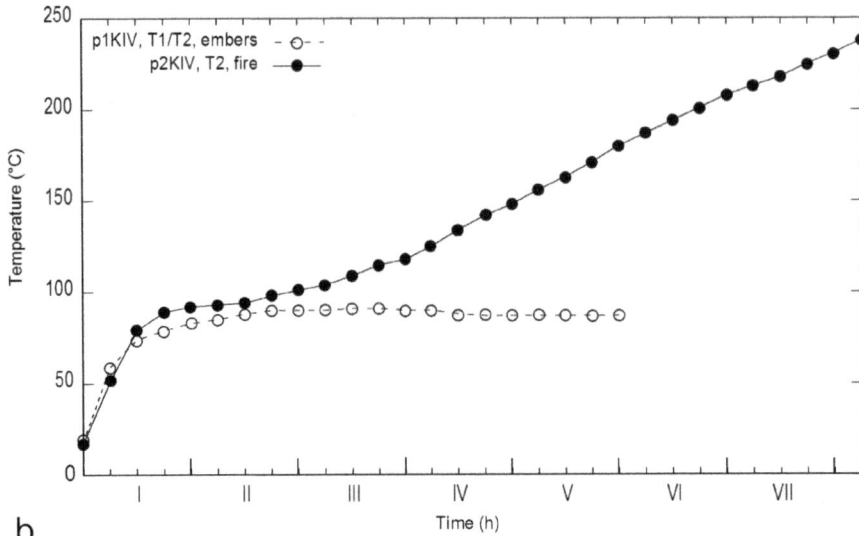

b

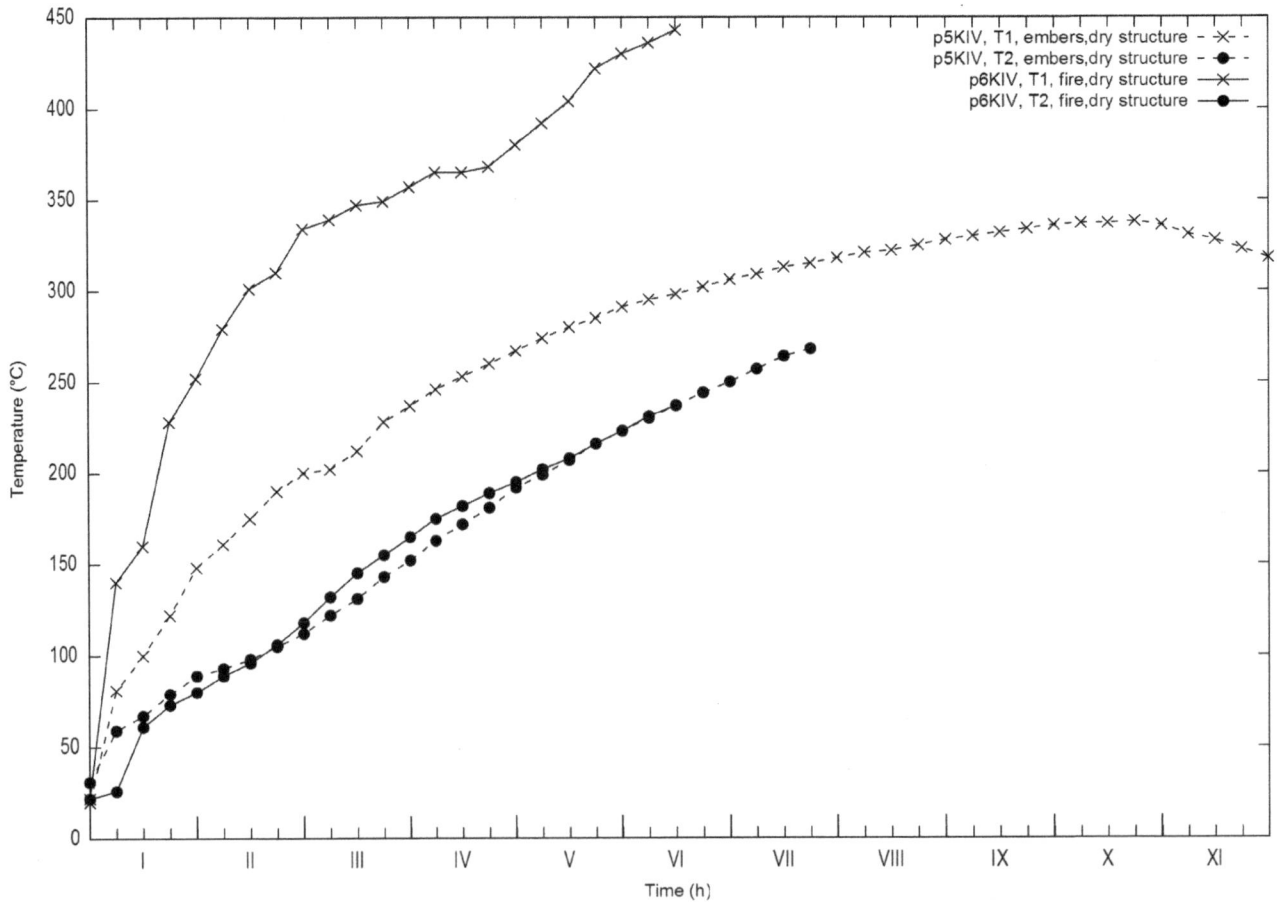

Fig. 7.1 A combined diagram of temperature distribution of forms fired by embers and fire.

Finally, summing up the subject of firing temperatures we can conclude that the highest temperature is reached in the clay fired after drying when direct fire is used. The maximum temperature readout in clay at point T1 (just under the surface) is 655.2°C (firing episode III), at point T2–483°C (firing episode II). Slightly lower temperature is reached by clay fired when still wet using direct fire. The maximum temperature at point T1/T2 is 484.8°C.

Even repeated firing of the form does not cause an increase in the temperature of the clay over 650°C, which temperature seems to be the limit for forms fired using direct fire.

Firing using embers causes the clay to heat to a much smaller extent. In case of firing of dried clay hearths the clay, during firing episode II, reached the maximum recorded temperature of T1–413.3°C, T2–313.8°C. The lowest value was noted when firing of wet clay hearth was done with embers.

Clay subjected to temperature over ca. 300°C, once it has lost its molecular water (Rice, 2005), will not longer dissolve in water when wetted and does not revert to its original state. It is worth noting at the same time that samples of clay taken in the cave are quick to disintegrate and fully dissolve reverting to their original state. After dissolving the obtained clay can be moulded again at will. However, analyses conducted by both Panagiotis Karkanas and by Maciej Pawlikowski demonstrate that clay from Klissoura had been subjected to temperature of 400–600°C (Pawlikowski, et al., 2000:23. Karkanas, et al., 2004:519–521;), and therefore the molecular water should have evaporated from these samples. Thus, it is feasible that clay hearths, while deposited in the ground, had come under such physical processes (freezing and thawing) and chemical processes (penetration of water) that the structure of the clay was subjected to such extreme disintegration that once immersed in water it disintegrates and becomes plastic. Even so it is puzzling that finds of analogous fragments of fired clay originating both from clay hearths and from animal figurines at Dolni Vestonice do not dissolve in water, what was emphasised by authors of the analyses (Vandiver, et al., 1989). Perhaps the specific condition of the substrate at site Klissoura causes such an extreme disintegration of the clay hearths.

At the same time it is worth noting at this point that the results of FTIR and DTA analyses proved that clay originating from different structures had been subjected to different temperatures. Analyses of Pawlikowski (Pawlikowski, et al., 2000) showed that clay had been subjected to temperature higher than 570°C, so we are allowed to conclude that it had been exposed to the action of fire rather than only to embers. Analyses of Karkanas (Karkanas, et al., 2004:519–521) showed that clay had been subjected to temperature ca. 400°C what would suggest heating the clay structure by embers. We can assume that it was irrelevant for the users whether the form is heated using direct fire or embers what would explain the differences in temperature. The other

possibility is that clay hearths were fired only in one way: either by using embers or direct fire and differences in temperature can be explained on the basis of experiments which show the substantial differences in temperature depending on the readout point in the clay structure.

Results: the process of oxidation of the clay

When a fire is made directly over the clay hearth found in the ground oxygen is free to flow only into the upper layers of the clay which causes the iron compounds to oxidise. Simultaneously, as with every firing of clay directly in open fire the surface of the clay develops blotches and discolourations of many hues. In the layer of clay in direct contact with the substrate the access of oxygen during firing is sufficiently limited for oxygen compounds to reduce producing a characteristic black hue. If the clay is fired in oxidising conditions and oxygen is cut off only at the end of firing then a characteristic grey hue appears on surface o the clay.

Reduction of iron compounds is not the only reason for the appearance of black hue in the ceramic mass. If during firing the ceramic paste contains a substantial quantity of organic matter and oxygen inflow is insufficient, then this matter is not subjected to complete combustion. In the cross–section of the clay hearth the edges of pores and spaces left by burnt out organic matter develop fine black spots.

The sequence of changes in the colour of the clay during successive experimental firing processes was as follows: first, the clay turned brown/dark brown, next it turned black at bottom only to become oxidised as time went by and beginning from the rim to take on a beige or red hue. However, the tendency was for it to remain black at the bottom. After several firing episodes in high temperature of over 400°C the clay hearth in cross section became bi–coloured–red on the top, black at the bottom.

The appearance of the clay hearths after experimental firing episodes did not correspond to the finds of prehistoric clay structures from the cave in case of which the clay each time had a deep reddish–brown or outright reddish hue without traces of black discolouration.

The author is inclined to conclude that it is impossible to fire over 100 structures in fully oxidising conditions, without obtaining the least trace of black hue. She is confirmed in her conviction by the fact that even the building of a new clay hearth over one used earlier and firing caused colour change in the clay hearth found underneath, and therefore one exposed to a much lower temperature. Analysing the distribution of the prehistoric clay hearths at the site and the fact of repeated overlapping of structures, it seems impossible that in relation to each of them all the rules favouring oxidation of clay had been used. The rules are as follows.

- Clay hearth is build over ashes or embers helping to increase oxygen inflow from below.

- The clay hearth is built over another also helping to increase oxygen inflow.
- The clay hearth is fired when still wet causing the clay hearth to crack and facilitates oxygen inflow.
- The clay hearth is fired using embers causing the clay to be fired only to a limited extent and not change its hue, but only when the clay is not heated to a temperature higher than ca. 300°C.
- The clay hearth is fired repeatedly for long hours, embers are removed during firing to ensure the access of oxygen to the entire surface of the clay hearth.

It seems unfeasible that the prehistoric features discovered at Klissoura had been treated in such an unusual manner, especially that, as was noted a number of times, the very fact of being found under a fired clay form may have an impact on reduction of the clay.

Assuming that these distinctive hearths must have served a specific purpose or purposes we may say that the manner of their use could have favoured the oxidation of the clay. But it still seems improbable that over 100 structures would not contain traces of even the slightest discolouration, especially if we take into consideration the appearance of already mentioned analogous structures from Dolni Vestonice (Vandiver, et al., 1989). If we nevertheless pursued the hypothesis that the clay hearths were used in a way, which increased the likelihood of the clay becoming oxidised, then we would have to adopt the assumptions presented here with regard to the conditions of firing.

CHAPTER 8

CONCLUSIONS: THE USES OF THE CLAY HEARTHS

To better understand the purpose of the clay hearths described in this publication we should answer the question: what is the difference between the two types of hearths found at the site, and above all, how do the properties of a hearth change once it has been given an underlying layer of clay:

A fire overlying a clay hearth is restricted in character which prevents the embers from spreading outside the hearth. The layer of clay prevents the fire from starting elsewhere and the ashes from spreading.

- The clay acts as insulation between the ground which may be cold and take up great amount of heat from the hearth and the fire itself. At the same time the clay heats very slowly but retains the heat for a long time; hearths with clay structures retain heat over for longer even when the fire has gone out. The deeper the clay hearth the better it is for conserving the embers after the fire has gone out.
- The contents of the fire burning on a clay hearth do not mix with the substrate which causes the resulting ashes to be without contamination from it. Additionally, there is a possibility of burying in the embers over the clay hearth objects which need heating and later remove them without danger of losing or soiling them (this applies especially to foodstuffs such as edible plant tubers). It seems more effective to bake them in the ashes or embers in a clay hearth because the clay represents an additional source of heat.
- The heated clay can be used like heated stones after the embers have been swept out.

As it was already mentioned phytoliths were very scarce in samples of ashes from above clay hearth in contrast to other samples of the same layer (Albert, 2010). Therefore we may conclude that clay structures were not left swept out because the ashes were not mixed with ashes from the same layer, hence the clay hearths must have been left filled with ashes.
On top of that almost no charcoals were found above clay hearths in contrast to family hearths, although the ashes were mostly wood ashes (Ntinou, 2010)

Ntinou's analyses (2010) showed that the distribution of identified wood species did not differ between flat hearts and clay hearths. The charcoals could have been transported then from the normal fireplaces to the clay structures (Ntinou, 2010)

However the amount of charcoals differed between samples taken from fireplaces and clay hearths. It may be concluded that the clay structures either were used in a way which augmented burning charcoals into ashes or the conditions in clay structures themselves improved the burning process e.g. by increasing the temperature of the fireplace.

The experiments do not provide us with clear results regarding the process of firing clay structures. However we may conclude that it was possible to avoid reduction of the clay when either the clay hearth was fired when still wet, or clay structure was fired using embers transported from another fireplace, or it was fired repeatedly for long hours. Removing embers during firing ensures access of oxygen to the entire surface of the clay hearth.

Reconstruction of the whole process

On the basis of experiments it was possible to reconstruct the sequence of activities associated with making and using the clay moulds. In this sequence were included also all the processes which may have had an impact on the clay form when it was in use and afterwards.

The general graphic diagram (fig.8.1) illustrates all the factors which have a bearing on the clay moulds, starting from method of preparing the raw clay through to the post depositional processes. It does not take into account different variants used to heat the clay or the uses of the clay structures; these area presented in a more detailed graphic sequence. In reconstructing all the activities and processes associated with the clay forms it is possible to distinguish five stages.

Stage I covers the preparation of the raw material and the place where the clay form is to be built; activities such as bringing the raw material to the cave (A1), preparing the clay to make into a form by adding water and working it (A2), preparing the place for the future clay form by digging a hole and clearing the surface (A3). On the diagram (fig.8.2) these activities are illustrated as a single stage because their sequence may have been subject to change.

State II covers the making of the form (B) in a location prepared earlier and, in some cases, leaving it to dry (C).

Stage III describes all the activities associated with firing the clay form that is, exposing it to high temperatures (D) and, in some cases, cleaning the upper surface of the clay form (E). That the clay hearths were fired in advance before they were used is only hypothetical. If this was so, then we have to assume that the use of these structures was connected with exposing them to high temperature.

But it is likely that the clay was subjected to firing before it started to be used irrespective of whether the fact of using it was connected to exposing it to a high temperature or not. If using the clay forms did not involve heating them then we need to assume that the forms may have been fired in advance.

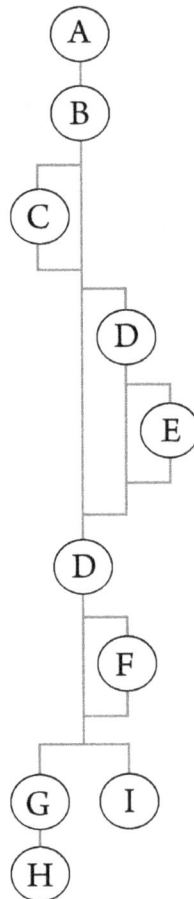

Fig. 8.1 General chaîne opératoire for the clay forms. A–preparation of the raw material and the place where the clay form is to be built, B–building the form (several possible methods), C–leaving the form to dry, D–firing the clay hearth (500–700°C), E–sweeping out the embers and sweeping the form clean, F–usage of the clay hearth, G–modelling a new structure over an older clay hearth, H–subjecting the clay hearth to high temperature by making a fire in an overlying clay form (100–200°C), I–gradual burying of the clay form by earth.

Stage IV covers activities associated with different uses of the forms: heating the clay form (D) and putting it to some use (F). The structures may have been used repeatedly.

The last stage (V) covers processes at work after the form went out of use. At this stage a new form would be positioned over an older one (G), as a result of which, the form would once again be exposed to the action of high temperature (H), or the form was filled with earth (I).

The general graphic sequence of activity can be expanded in detailed basing on input from experiments performed and presents possible scenarios of using this sort of ceramic structure.

Heating a clay structure, both at the stage of firing and when it was used could have been achieved either by building an open fire over it (D1), or what is more probable by spreading over it hot embers (D2). After heating the form its use could have involved using the fire made over the clay form (F2), or possibly, using the clay form itself (F1) and its thermic properties which made it possible e.g., to store hot embers over a longer period. The forms could have been used over and over again and the cycle of heating them could have been repeated. A clay form no longer in use would come under post depositional processes described earlier.

Hypotheses of the uses of the clay hearths

On the basis of the analysis of the clay hearths, the experiments results and the review of analogous clay structures it seems reasonable, therefore, to put forward three hypotheses regarding the possible uses of the prehistoric clay hearths at Klissoura. All the hypotheses are based on the use of thermal properties of heated clay or specific properties of the concave form of the clay hearths.

1. The results of experiments of the IV series demonstrated quite clearly that the clay hearths favour the storage of embers from a fire for a long time. A structure of small dimensions (diameter of ca. 30cm and depth of a few centimetres) makes it possible to store embers for longer than 24 hours. These properties of the hearth could have been used during the Palaeolithic and hearths of the described type could have served as places in which fire was stored while the people were away from the camp site (fig.8.2.a1 and b1).

2. Having a clay hearth under the fire makes it more convenient to cover foodstuffs by ashes and embers. The layer of clay at bottom made it easier to take them out after cooking and was an additional source of heat. At the same time, hearths with a clay lining, because they retained heat for a long time, made it possible to bury in the embers this kind of objects which need to be heated for a long time. As such a fire burning in a clay hearth makes it possible to keep objects in a temperature of around 300–400°C (a prehistoric cooking oven), (fig.8.2.a2 and b2).

5. A fire left to burn itself out over a clay understructure produces ashes which have the advantage over ashes of an ordinary hearth that they were not mixed with the underlying ground and were very easy to remove from the clay hearth. Such ashes could have been used in preserving foodstuffs, mainly meat. The meat could have been cured within the clay hearths themselves by being placed in the ashes. This last hypothesis assumes that the clay hearths were used for ash production (fig.8.2.a1 and b1).

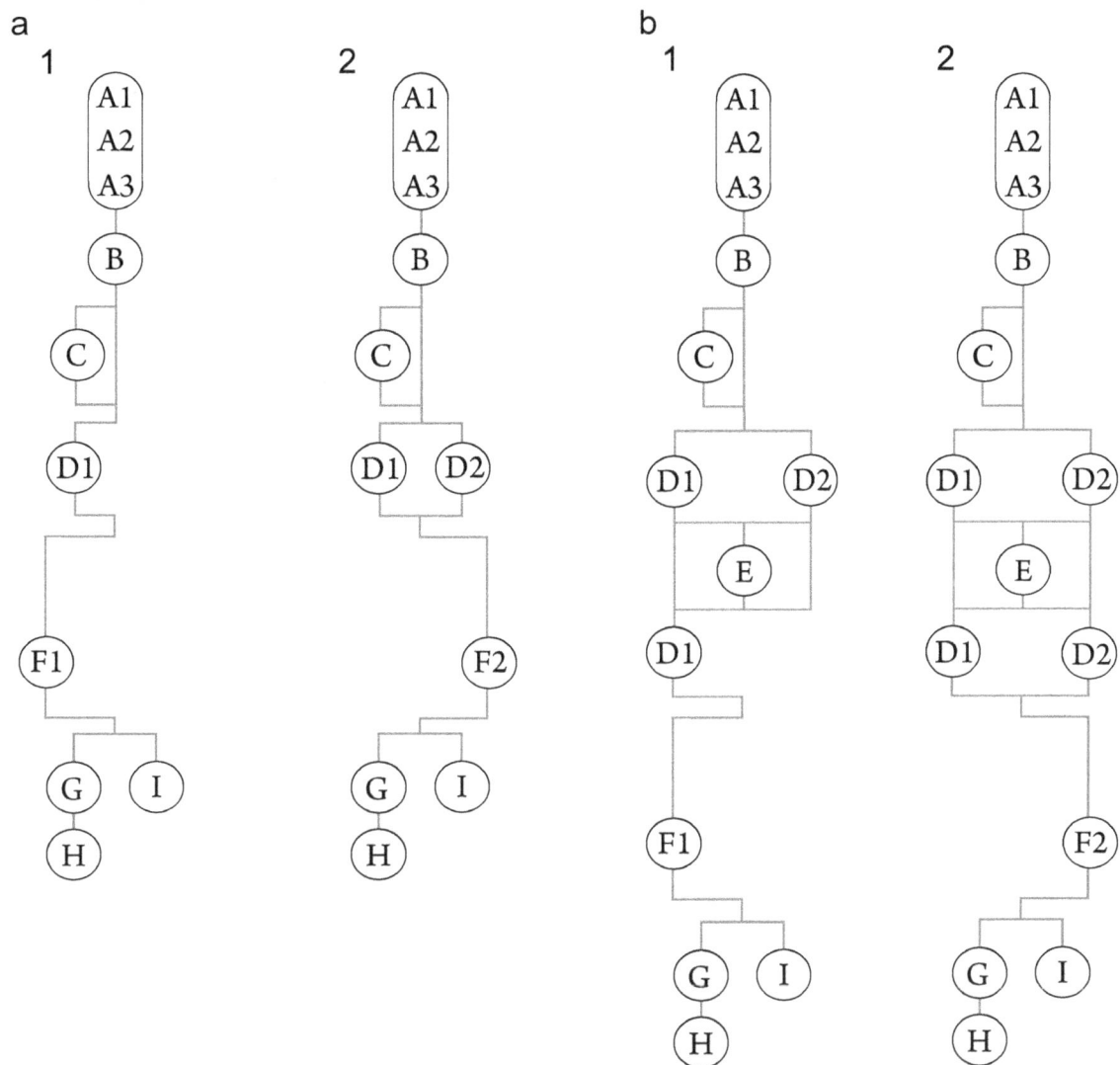

Fig. 8.2 Schemes showing hypothetical ways of using clay structures. a) Schemes without firing clay structures before using them, b) the schemes with firing the clay structure before using. Numbers refers to the hypothetical ways of using the clay structure (in text). Key to the scheme: A1–obtaining and transporting clay to the cave A2–adding water and working the clay, A3–preparing the location for the clay hearth, B–building the form (several possible methods), C–leaving the form to dry, D1–making a fire over the clay hearth (500–700°C), D2–piling embers onto the form (400–500°C), E–sweeping out the embers and sweeping the form clean, F1–using the clay form itself and its thermic properties e.g. leaving the fire to smoulder, keeping the embers, possibly, moving them elsewhere to make a new fire using the clay hearth, F2–using the fire made over the clay form, G–modelling a new structure over an older clay hearth, H–subjecting the clay hearth to the action of temperature again by making a fire in an overlying clay form (100–200°C), I–gradual burying of the clay form by earth.

The hypothesis considered in some experiments of the first, second and third series of placing foodstuffs or other objects on a heated and swept clean clay structure or boiling water in it has to be rejected. It is undermined by the fact that after use the clay hearth was supposedly swept clean of ashes. However the majority of prehistoric clay hearths at Klissoura were overlain by a layer of ashes. At the same time wind could not transport the ashes from places they pile up into all manners or hollow, concave structures. Such a process is not confirmed by analyses of charcoals and phytoliths quoted above.

During the experiments, if the form had been swept clean in the evening the next day the clay was covered by a fine layer of ashes. It seems therefore that the post–depositional processes may have been responsible for the accumulation of wind–blown ashes within the concave surface of the clay hearths, which has been observed in trench sections over the clay structures. On the basis of

59

those results we may conclude that the forms were left filled with ashes.

Epilogue

Even though the clay hearths occurred in Upper Palaeolithic layers over a substantial depth of more than 1.8m the structures do not exhibit statistically significant differences in their metric attributes. At the same time analysis of spatial distribution of the clay hearths demonstrated that successive structures were established at a same spot over and over again spanning a depth of as much as several score centimetres. At first the clay hearths grouped in the northern area of the trench directly by the stone wall. With time the location of the clay hearths changed and they were established in the southern area of the trench. The fact of the occurrence of two types of hearths at the site definitely proves that hearths with clay substructures served a specific purpose. It is likely that this purpose was associated with using specific characteristics of a hearth made over a layer of clay or was connected to the use of the concave clay hearth itself. In the present text we have signalled only a few possible methods of using this type of clay structures. It is possible that their function was entirely different still.

The key to understanding the function of the clay hearths may be in precisely specifying the methods used to fire these structures. Clay forms discovered during excavation had over their entire surface and in cross–section a rusty–red hue which testifies to firing in oxidising conditions. Archaeological experiments carried out by the author demonstrated that during firing of analogous clay hearths it is not possible to fully control the oxygen conditions, and consequently, the colour of the clay hearth. It is possible to obtain a rusty–red hue of the clay hearth only in a few special cases, but we may assume that during the Upper Palaeolithic the colour of the clay hearth was not a factor which influenced the process of firing during its use. At the same time the experiments demonstrated that the clay in the clay hearth subjected to high temperature heats very unevenly. The difference in temperature during firing of the layer of clay directly affected by fire and the bottom of the clay hearth in contact with the ground is ca. 200°C. The temperature of the clay even during repeated firing does not exceed 650°C, which confirms the results of the earlier analyses of the temperature of firing of the original clay hearths (Karkanas, et al., 2004:519–521, Pawlikowski, et al., 2000:23).

BIBLIOGRAPHY

Albert, R.M. Hearths and plant uses during the Upper Palaeolithic period at Klissoura Cave 1 (Greece): the results from phytolith analyses, in Koumouzelis, Kozłowski, Stiner (eds): 71-86.

Hachi, S., Frohlich, F., Gendron–Badou, A., De Lumley, H., Roubet, C. & S. Abdessadok. 2002. Upper Palaeolithic cooked clay figurines from Afalou Bou Rhummel (Babors, Algeria). First Infra–red absorption spectroscopic analyses, *L'Anthropologie*, 106: 57–97.

Kaczanowska, M. Kozłowski, J.K. & K. Sobczyk. 2010. Upper Palaeolithic human occupations and material culture at Klissoura Cave 1, in Koumouzelis, Kozłowski, Stiner (eds): 133-286.

Karkanas, P., Koumouzelis, M., Kozłowski, J.K., Sitlivy, V., Sobczyk, K., Berna, F. & S. Weine. 2004. The earliest evidence for clay hearths: Aurignacian features in Klissoura Cave southern Greece, *Antiquity* 78: 513–525.

Karkanas, P. 2010. Geology, stratigraphy and site formation processes of the Upper Palaeolithic and later sequence in Klissoura Cave 1, in Koumouzelis, Kozłowski, Stiner (eds): 15-36.

Koumouzelis M., Kozłowski, J.K. & M.C. Stiner. 2010. *Klissoura Cave 1, Argolid, Greece: the Upper Palaeolithic sequence.* Eurasian Prehistory 7(2).

Kuhn, S. L.2010. Radiocarbon dating results for the Early Upper Paleolithic of Klissoura Cave 1, in Koumouzelis, Kozłowski, Stiner (eds): 37-46.

Kot M. 2008a. Structured Aurignacian clay–hearths from Klissoura Cave in Greece. The reconstruction of making, burning and using clay structures in Upper Palaeolithic, *Journal of Experimental Pyrotechnologies* 1: 47–50.

Kot M. 2008b. Badania eksperymentalne górnopaleolitycznych struktur glinianych, *Rocznik Studenckiego Ruchu Naukowego Uniwersytetu Warszawskiego* 6: 43–60.

Koumouzelis, M., Ginter, B., Kozłowski, J.K., Pawlikowski, M., Bar–Yosef, O., Albert, R.M., Lityńska–Zając, M., Stworzewicz, E., Wojtal, P., Lipecki, G., Tomek, T., Bocheński, Z.M. & A. Pazdur 2001a. The Early Upper Palaeolithic In Greece: The Excavations In Klissoura Cave, *Journal of Archaeological Science* 28: 515–539.

Koumouzelis M., Kozłowski J.K., Escutenaire C., Sitlivy V., Sobczyk K., Valladas H., Tisnerat–Laborde N., Wojtal P. & B. Ginter. 2001b. La Fin Du Paleolithique Moyen Et Le Debut Du Paleolitique Superieur En Grece: La Sequence De La Grotte 1 De Klissoura. *L'Anthropologie* 105: 469–504.

March R., Ferreri, J.C. & C. Guez. 1993. Étude des foyers préhistoriques des gisements magdaléniens du Bassin parisien : l'approche expérimentale, *Mémoires GASM* 1: 87-95

March, R., Muhieddine, M. & É. Canot. 2010. Simulation 3D des structures de combustion préhistoriques, *Proceedings of Virtual Retrospect 2009* 4: 19-29

Meignen, L., Bar-Yosef, O., Goldberg, P., & S. Weiner. 2001. Le feu au Paleolithique moyen: recherches sur les structures de combustion et le statut des foyers. L'exemple du Proche-Orient. *Paleorient* 26: 9–22.

Ntinou, M. 2010. Wood charcoal analysis at Klissoura Cave 1 (Prosymna, Peloponese): the Upper Palaeolithic vegetation, in Koumouzelis, Kozłowski, Stiner (eds): 47-70.

Pawlikowski, M., Koumouzelis, M., Ginter, B. & J.K. Kozłowski. 2000. Emerging ceramics technology in structured Aurignacian earths in the Klissoura Cave in Greece, *Archaeology Ethnology and Anthropology of Eurasia* 4: 19–29.

Rice, P.M. 2005. *Pottery Analysis.* Chicago and London: The University of Chicago Press.

Starkovich, B.M. & M.C. Stiner, 2010. Upper Palaeolithic animal exploitation at Klissoura Cave 1 in Southern Greece: dietary trends and mammal taphonomy, in Koumouzelis, Kozłowski, Stiner (eds): 107-132.

Starkovich, B.M. 2011. Trends In Subsistence From The Middle Paleolithic Through Mesolithic At Klissoura Cave 1 (Peloponnese, Greece)/ Unpublished PhD thesis, Faculty of The School Of Anthropology, The University Of Arizona.

Vandiver P.B., Soffer, O., Klima, B. & J. Svoboda. 1989. The Origins of Ceramic Technology at Dolni Věstonice, Czechoslovakia, *Science* 4933:1002–1008.

Walker, P.L. & K.P. Miller. 2005. Time, temperature, and oxygen availability: an experimental study of the effects of environmental conditions on the color and organic content of cremated bone, *American Journal of Physical Anthropology*, Supplement 40: 216–217.

Walker, P.L., Miller, K.W.P. & R. Richman. 2008. Time, temperature, and oxygen availability: an experimental study of the effects of environmental conditions on the color and organic content of cremated bone, in C.W. Schmidt & S.A. Symes (ed.), *The Analysis of Burned Human Remains*, 129–135. London: Academic Press.

62

Plate 1. 1) Bicoloured section of clay structure (p2RIII after single firing episode); 2) Red–beige section with black spaces around the burnt out particles of organic matter (p5KII after the second firing); 3) Red section of clay structure moulded on embers (p2KII after the single firing episode); 4) Section of the substrate affected by the fire (j2RIII after the single firing episode); 5) Clay hallow affected by fire (j2RIII after the single firing episode);6) section of the substrate affected by the fire (j2RIII after the single firing episode);

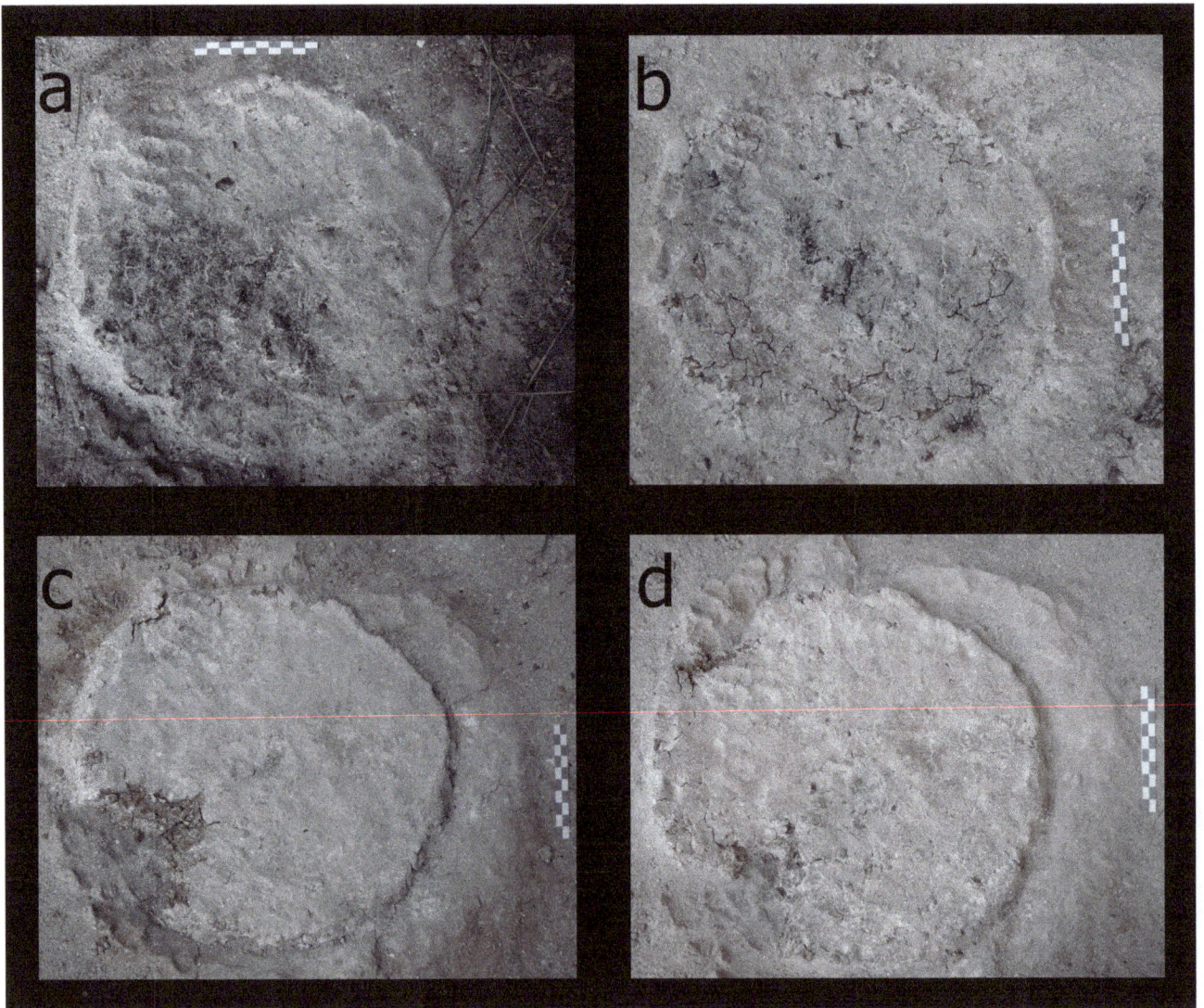

Plate 2. 1) Dark-red section of a clay structure (p4KIV after the fourth firing episode); 2) Red cracked section of a clay structure (p2KIV after the fourth firing episode); 3) p2KIV from the top after each firing episode.

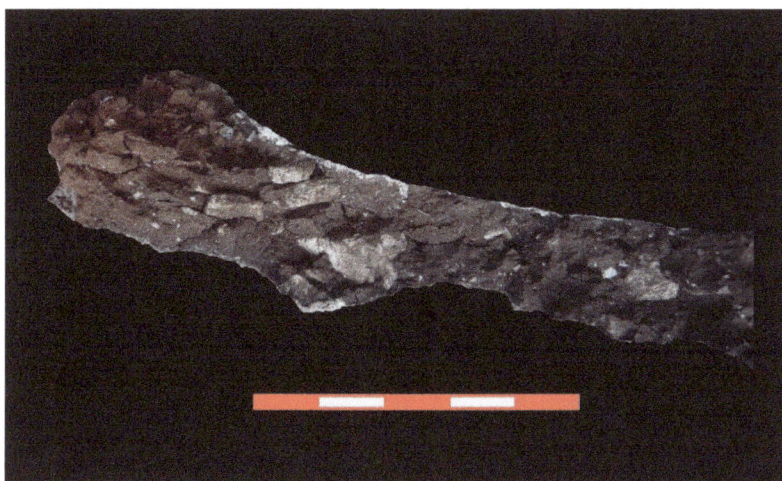

Plate 3. 1) Bicoloured section of clay structure (p7KIV after the fourth firing episode); 2) The underside of p7KIV after the fourth firing episode 3) Section of a clay structure which became red next to the rimb and dark brown in a centre (p6KIV after the fourth firing episode); 4) Bicoloured section of clay structure (p9KIV after the second firing episode); 5 Bicoloured section of clay structure (p14KIV after the second firing episode).